Four in One

By Scott and Bonna Brooks

Available at www.BrooksFamilyStore.com

ISBN 978-0-692-80796-5

Copyright ©2016 TX 8-212-533

Table of Contents

Table of Contents (Continued)

Dedication

We dedicate this *Four in One* book to you the reader and also to Jesus. May the Holy Spirit use this book to grow you all the more into a wonderful friendship with Jesus. And may that friendship positively affect all of your other friendships as well.

Introduction by Scott and Bonna Brooks

There are four books combined into this *Four in One* book:

> **Book 1:** *Twos and Threes*
>
> **Book 2:** *Would you like to see an Amazing Miracle?*
>
> **Book 3:** *Deeper Friendships*
>
> **Book 4:** *At His Feet*

These four books work together as a single unit with some concepts more fully explained in some of the books than in others. So, even though each of the four books is published and available separately, we thought it would benefit you to have all four books combined into this *Four in One* book, including having them in the correct order. We thought this would be better than you having one of the four books and trying to figure out how it ties to the other three books, or trying to locate a copy of any of the books that you are missing.

Even though we recommend reading the books in order, there is one exception. If you struggle with knowing that God exists, then we would recommend that you first read *Would you like to see an Amazing Miracle?* (Book 2), because in that book there are instructions that give easy steps for you to take so that there will be a very high percentage chance that you will get to see a miracle with your own eyes – which will let you know for sure that Jesus (who is God) is alive and is doing miracles today!

When I, Scott, first became a Christian after living the first twenty years of my life as an atheist, I would have loved to have a copy of this *Four in One* book! Instead, it took me **many** years of reading the Bible and looking to learn from Jesus in all of life, in order to learn the many things that are explained in this book. At one point, my son David shared how it had taken three months for him to learn the latest thing Jesus was teaching him. I then shared with David that the same thing took me three years – and that unlike David, I did not have anyone at that time who could explain to me what I was in the midst of learning – which in turn could have helped me to learn it much more quickly, just like David did. So, if this book helps you to learn these things **much** quicker than it has taken me, then I am excited for you! And I hope these things become at least as valuable to you as they have become to me!

I, Bonna, contributed only a little to writing **Would you like to see an Amazing Miracle?** (Book 2). But, I have read all four books many times! You might think that I would master the material after a single read. But, similar to reading the Bible, each time I read them, the Holy Spirit makes new things stand out to me and in turn helps me to grow all the more as a Christian. Not only do I learn new things, but I also really enjoy reading about such things as the wonderfulness of Jesus! I especially like to look at the character and desires of God that are so important that they are listed four times in this **Four in One** book, and God has used my reading of those characteristics and desires to build a stronger foundation for my entire Christian life. I hope you are as helped and blessed by the material in this **Four in One** book as I have and continue to be!

The Gospel

All four books contained in **Four in One** give an explanation of the Gospel – with the greatest details being in **Deeper Friendships** (Book 3). Since the Gospel is so incredibly important, we thought it would be good to now share it with you one additional time, but first taking a look at how the Gospel is often shared from a judicial standpoint instead of from the better and fuller context found in the Bible that explains it from a relational standpoint. To us, the Gospel makes so much more sense from a relational standpoint! So, we hope you find this section about the Gospel to be informative, encouraging, and of value to you.

From a judicial standpoint, the Gospel can sound like this:

> A man took his son and beat him up so that the man could be nice to the other children in the neighborhood.

In this metaphor, the man is God the Father, the son is Jesus, the Father beat-up Jesus on the Cross (i.e. death by crucifixion), and we are the children in the neighborhood. If I, Scott, was a non-Christian and someone shared the Gospel with me in such a way, I would think that the Father is unloving and therefore would probably conclude that I would not want anything to do with Him.

The Gospel is also shared from a judicial standpoint by a person using a courtroom metaphor where they share about a person who is on trial and God the Father is the judge. The person is found to be guilty. But, Jesus then steps in out of His love for the person and takes the punishment for the person so that the person is then free to go. But from this judicial perspective, it is harder for the non-Christian to understand why they would be guilty in the first place.

The Gospel is often shared from a judicial standpoint and with such a high level summary that it does not make sense to the non-Christian. The following is an example of a one sentence judicial summary.

> "If you do not accept Jesus into your heart, you are going to Hell!"

We (Bonna and Scott) were once taking a walk and a conversation arose with a young woman who was a non-Christian. She told us that once a Baptist pastor walked into the room that she and her friends were in, and he proceeded to tell them that they were going to Hell because they had not accepted Jesus into their hearts. The young woman proceeded to say that it did not make any sense to them that "not accepting Jesus into their hearts" would doom them to Hell. We then shared how the Gospel is often shared from this judicial standpoint rather than the more relational standpoint found in the

Bible, and then proceeded to explain the differences to her. At the end of the discussion, she was not yet ready to become a Christian, but she thanked us for explaining it to her and gave each of us a hug before we went our separate ways.

So from a one sentence judicial standpoint, the Gospel can sound like the following to the non-Christian.

> "If you do not accept my invitation to have dinner with me, I am going to take you to court and get you thrown into jail!"

If someone said this to us, we would most likely consider it an unloving invitation to say the least! And just from the demanding tone of it, we would be inclined to decline their offer.

Since the Gospel from a judicial perspective does not make as much sense as from a relational perspective, some people who share it judicially, water it down to present it as a free ticket to Heaven instead of as an ongoing friendship with Jesus – where it will only work if the person is very committed to Jesus as their top priority. Jesus summarized the needed level of commitment as:

> Then he (Jesus) said to them all: "Whoever wants to be my disciple must deny themselves and take up their cross daily and follow me." (Luke 9:23)

Instead of watering down the Gospel, others do include the "cost of being a disciple", but since it is less attractive judicially, they put a heavy demand upon people to try to force them to receive it. They may become so demanding that they yell at people from street corners! But this pushy approach can give the idea to non-Christians that since the person is so pushy, therefore the God they represent must be pushy too. In other words, the person sharing the Gospel does not reflect God's character of love where love does not demand its own way.

> **Love is** patient and kind. Love is not jealous or boastful or proud or rude. **It does not demand its own way**. It is not irritable, and it keeps no record of being wronged. It does not rejoice about injustice but rejoices whenever the truth wins out. Love never gives up, never loses faith, is always hopeful, and endures through every circumstance. (1 Corinthians 13:4-7 NLT, emphasis ours)

All of these judicial approaches tend to miss the mark since they first start with details about justice rather than starting with God's love and His valuing of people's freewill. So, if we start from a relational standpoint where God indeed loves people and in that love values their freewill to accept or reject relationship with Him, then the Gospel makes lots of sense! This includes the judicial aspects (such as Jesus' payment for sins on the Cross) that are best understood within a relational context.

What follows is an explanation of the Gospel from a relational standpoint that makes use of a diagram not found in the other four books. Over the years, Jesus helped us to expand the diagram to include additional details to better clarify certain points.

We have used this diagram numerous times to explain the Gospel to non-Christians. We have also used it to help Christians gain a better understanding of the Gospel as well. When we share it, we draw part of the diagram, explain it, draw more, explain more, etc. So, when we share the diagram and explanations with you, we will share it as if we were drawing it out and sharing it with a non-Christian in real-time dialogue so that you can get a feel of how it would flow conversationally. And each time we add to the diagram, we will **bold** the new part so that you can distinguish it from what was drawn before. We will then explain the new **bolded** part.

It has been great to see Jesus use the diagram to help quite a number of people to come into relationship with Him (i.e. their becoming Christians). And we welcome you to pray and ask Jesus to help you to know if it would ever be a good time for you to use the diagram in some way with others.

Diagram 1:

Diagram 1 Explained:

God has perfect love for you and as such gives you the freewill choice to receive His love and to enter into a friendship with Him or to reject His love and friendship offer. If you decide to use your freewill to receive God's love and friendship offer, then the question becomes, "How can you actually do this?"

One approach people take is to try to be "good enough" for God, thinking that if they do enough good things, that once they die, God will have to accept them into some form of Heaven – which is called different names in different religions, such as Heaven, Nirvana, or the Celestial Kingdom. But, will this approach work?

Diagram 2:

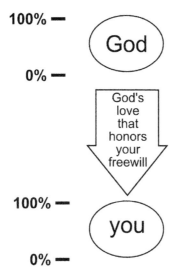

Diagram 2 Explained:

In terms of perfection, how good do you think God is?

And in terms of perfection, how good do you think you are?

Diagram 3:

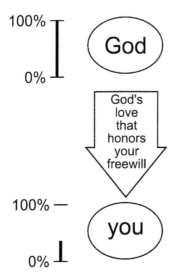

Diagram 3 Explained:

Most people correctly guess that God is at 100%. And they guess that they are somewhere between 10% and 80% depending on how good they feel they have been overall. And almost always, no one guesses that they are at 100%.

Diagram 4:

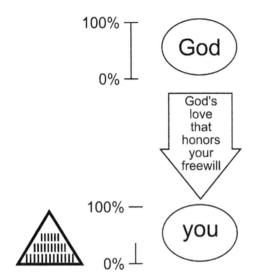

Diagram 4 Explained:

Most religions have a set of rules, and even build rules upon rules upon rules describing what a person would need to do in order to be "good enough". And people diligently try to follow those rules hoping that if they indeed do them well enough, that they will hopefully get to a high enough percentage to qualify. And some people believe in reincarnation and hope to be "good enough" after trying to improve over many lifetimes.

So, if you took this approach of trying to be "good enough", do you think you would be able to make it to 100%?

From a relational standpoint, it is clear that even if a person took incredible effort and did many things to be "good enough", they would still not make it to 100% and automatically qualify, because being "good enough" does not equate to relationship.

Could you imagine a man deciding that if for ninety days he would send a woman flowers (even roses), cards, and chocolates that at the end of the ninety days he would automatically be married to her? She would most likely not agree with his conclusion, and instead would prefer to be asked for her hand in marriage and given the freewill to say "I do" or not.

So, if this trying to be "good enough" approach does not work, then what will actually work?

Diagram 5:

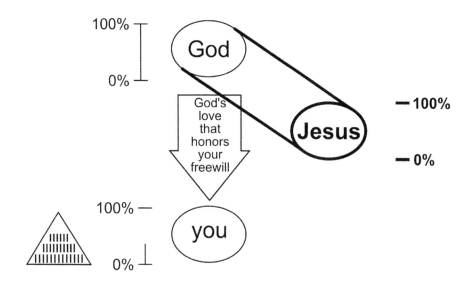

Diagram 5 Explained:

From a relational perspective, if we start with God's incredible love for people, then we find that He made a solution that would demonstrate His incredible love for people and in this it would honor their freewill to accept His love and friendship offer or to reject it.

The first step in God's solution was for Him to take on human form with the name Jesus, and to live on earth over 2,000 years ago in the first century. Since Jesus was fully God and fully human, He radiated God's love to every person that He interacted with.

Since Jesus was both fully God and fully human, what percentage do you think He was at in terms of His level of goodness?

Diagram 6:

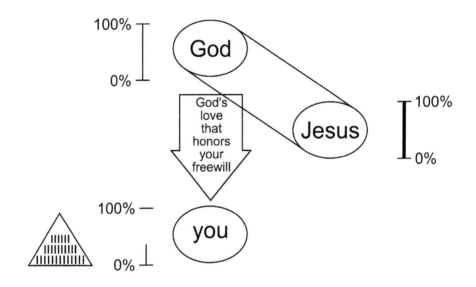

Diagram 6 Explained:

Jesus was at 100%.

And Jesus being at 100% was needed for God's amazing solution to occur.

Diagram 7:

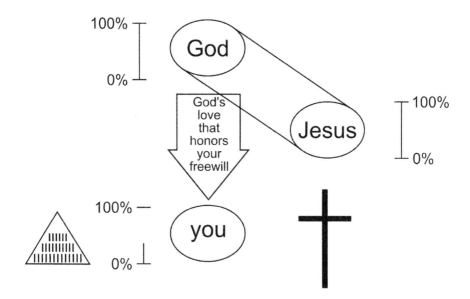

Diagram 7 Explained:

The second step in God's solution was for Him in the person of Jesus to go through a tremendous suffering out of His tremendous love for all people. The way this came about was through a sequence of events which started with Jesus being so loving toward people that He became very popular among the common people. In turn, the governing officials became very jealous of Jesus' incredible popularity. They also hated Jesus saying He was God. So, in their desire to remove Jesus' influence, they decided to kill Jesus by having Him executed by crucifixion – which was a painful death penalty used in that day, where they would hang a person on a cross until the person died.

Diagram 8:

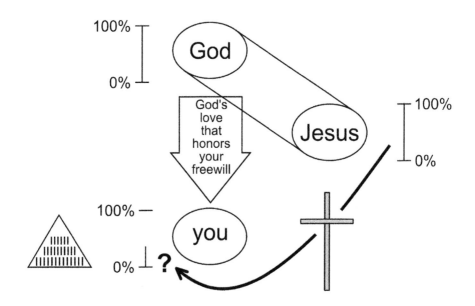

Diagram 8 Explained:

So, even though God could have easily prevented the crucifixion from happening, out of His incredible love for us, He allowed it to occur so that an incredibly amazing trade happened at the Cross that would provide what is needed for you to receive God's friendship offer!

On one side of the trade, Jesus became a blood sacrifice to pay for all of the relational violations (i.e. sins) we have done that have worked against the greatest two commandments to love God and to love our neighbors as ourselves. In other words, Jesus paid for all the things that would get in the way of us having better friendships with Him and each other. And when Jesus rose from the dead, it showed that His payment was fully complete. In other words, no further payment is needed.

On the other side of the trade, Jesus offers His perfection to us as a gift! This is amazing since through your efforts, you could never get to the 100% goodness level, and yet because of God's love for you, Jesus offers His 100% to you as a gift!

God still honors your freewill choice, so the question is whether or not you would like to receive Jesus' 100% as a gift. But if you indeed are willing to receive it, then it will qualify you to be able to also receive His Holy Spirit within you, where instead of God being far away from you, He instead is willing to dwell within you – which is the biggest key for you to grow in excellent friendships with Him and others, because it is His awesome power on the inside of you helping you all the time!

So, if all of this made sense to you and you decide it is what you would like to do, then one final thing is needed in order for you to receive it. And that is that you would need to be willing to commit your life to God so that He can work to free you up into doing well in your friendship with Him, which in turn will positively affect your friendships with others. It is similar to getting married. If a marriage relationship is going to work well, then both sides will need to grow and change. God is already perfect and therefore is in no need of change. But for us, changes are needed in order for us to grow in a privileged partnership of friendship with God.

Fortunately, God is smarter than we can imagine and knows better than we do on how we can best grow in love for Him, others, and ourselves. God taking us through this is not an easy process, but well worth it in terms of the wonderful relationships He can bring about.

Diagram 9:

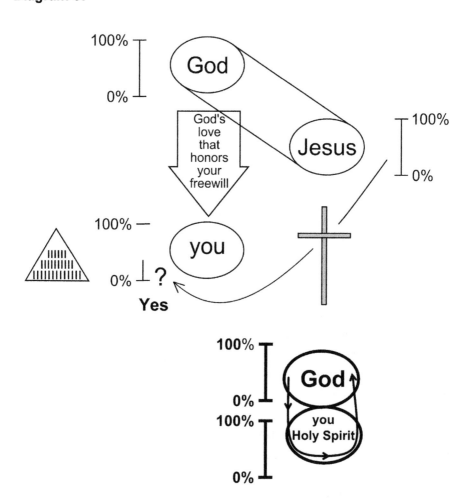

Diagram 9 Explained:

So, if you decide that you would like to commit your life to God, (including turning away from anything that would work against you loving God, others, and yourself), and you would like to receive His love and friendship offer to you, then He will do all of the following for you:

1. He will forgive you for **all** the relational violations you have ever done according to His payment for you on the Cross.

2. He will give you His 100% perfection as a gift.

3. He will give you His Holy Spirit to dwell within you and to help you in all of life to grow in excellent friendships with Him and others.

So, would you like to commit your life to God and receive His love and friendship offer to you?

If "yes", then the way to receive it is to ask, where you could say out loud or silently in your heart/mind the following:

Dear Jesus,

I commit my life fully to You so that You can grow me as an excellent friend to You and to others as well.

I thank You for dying for me on the Cross and paying for every relational violation that I have ever done.

I ask that You would forgive me according to Your payment for me on the Cross and that You would come to live and work inside of me through Your Holy Spirit.

Lastly, I ask that You would fill me with a tremendous measure of Your Holy Spirit and help me to grow well in my friendship with You, having Your love become the basis for me to better love You, others, and myself.

Thanks and in Jesus' name,

Your Name

We are so grateful that Jesus took the time to die on the Cross for all of us – including you! So, if in the past or just now you took this step, then we congratulate you on your excellent choice! And we hope that Jesus uses the rest of the material in this *Four in One* book to help you to grow well in your friendships with Him and with others too!

Thoughts about the Diagram

What is nice about the Gospel from a relational perspective is that it makes so much more sense both to non-Christians and to Christians. So, we hope you found this diagram and explanation to be helpful to you in seeing the Gospel all the more clearly from a relational perspective instead of from a judicial perspective.

In *Deeper Friendships* (Book 3) there are additional details about the Gospel including an in-depth look at what occurred on the Cross – which we are so very thankful for!

A Brief Overview of each of the Four Books

Overall, the four books are designed to help you to grow in a relational view of the Christian life where your friendships with Jesus and others can blossom in excellent ways!

To give you a better idea of how the four books fit together into this *Four in One* book, the following is a high level overview that skips **many** details, but still gives you the overall flow. Hopefully this "map" of the four books will help you as you read them.

Book 1: *Twos and Threes*

Even though *Twos and Threes* was written last, and as such builds upon the other three books, we still recommend that you read it first. There are two reasons for this. The first is that it is written standalone enough, with the concepts explained in enough detail, so that you can read it without having to first read the other three books. The second reason is because we have seen Jesus use *Twos and Threes* to free people up to be able to more easily gain the great benefits of twos and threes heart-to-heart fellowship, which in turn can make it much easier for them to both understand and benefit from the other three books.

This second reason is reflected in the dedication of **Twos and Threes** which gives the overall purpose of the book:

> "I dedicate this book to you the reader – especially if you have longed for better fellowship but have not been able to find it. May Jesus use this book and work in your life to bring you to wonderful friendships of true heart-to-heart fellowship!"

Twos and Threes then gives many practical ways for you to be able to gain more 2s-and-3s fellowship than you currently are partaking of, including the appendix which gives you easy, step-by-step instructions for how you can host your own **Twos and Threes Party** so that you can not only gain more heart-to-heart fellowship for yourself, but so that you can also provide this for others as well.

Book 2: *Would you like to see an Amazing Miracle?*

Many people have never seen a miracle, and therefore some of them may wonder at times if God truly exists or not. But if they do the leg-grow-out miracle steps outlined in the book, then there is a very high percentage chance that they will get to see their first miracle! In turn, it can provide them with this key piece of information for knowing that Jesus is risen, alive today, and doing miracles! What is great about this is that Jesus is doing this miracle a very high percentage of the time, so it can provide even an atheist with evidence that Jesus truly is alive! The book then explains who this invisible God is who does such miracles and it then introduces the Gospel to the reader, including explaining what is entailed in such a friendship (including the cost of daily picking up one's cross), and how they can enter into such a friendship with Jesus.

Please note that you do not have to try the leg-grow-out miracle to benefit from the book. But, we would still recommend that you try it anyway, since it is a wonderful thing to see, and it will also provide you with the valuable information of knowing that Jesus still performs miracles!

The book ends by suggesting that you next read *Deeper Friendships* (Book 3) since it gives additional details in what we have found to be very helpful in a life of friendship with God.

Book 3: *Deeper Friendships*

Deeper Friendships begins with a story of what it would be like to eat a meal with Jesus – including all of the wonderful friendship qualities that would be seen at such a table!

Deeper Friendships then looks at very root issues pertaining to both friendships with Jesus and with each other. It addresses such foundational questions as:

~ What is love?

~ What is the basis for us to value ourselves, others, and God?

~ What is sin?

~ What does God truly want from and for us?

Depending on how one answers these questions can have a very large difference on the quality of friendships the person has with both Jesus and others as well.

Deeper Friendships also provides insight into the amazing sacrifice that Jesus made for each of us on the Cross, and shows how God is not a distant God, but instead is One who knows firsthand the pain of the relational violations we have experienced! It also shows how Jesus is so selfless in His love for us that He first wants our best – no matter the cost to Himself!

Deeper Friendships ends by suggesting that you take the time to read ***At His Feet*** (Book 4) as a next step, since ***At His Feet*** provides many practical suggestions for how you can grow in your friendship with Jesus, which in turn will greatly help you to grow in your friendships with others as well.

Book 4: *At His Feet*

At His Feet has many practical suggestions for how to grow in your friendship with Jesus.

At His Feet looks at the issue of whether or not you have the ownership of your Christian life, and shows that if you delegate your Christian life to others (even those that seem more knowledgeable), that in the long run it will hinder your spiritual growth.

At His Feet also looks at a number of potentially challenging Bible passages, but from a relational perspective that can help you to not get tripped up by those passages, but to find lots of value in them instead.

At His Feet has an entire chapter titled, "A Priority of Time", which looks at how you view your time and the correlation to how that can help or hinder your Christian growth.

At His Feet ends with an appendix that provides practical suggestions on how you can read the Bible to get lots of value out of the Bible as a wonderful resource!

Conclusion

We are excited to have all four books available to you in this ***Four in One*** book!

We hope you found this introduction to be helpful in taking a further look at the Gospel, and that the overview of each of the four books has given you a good overall "map" as you now get to explore the details of each of the four books.

Overall, we hope ***Four in One*** becomes a major resource and valued treasure for you that Jesus uses in your life in wonderful ways!

With Jesus' love,

Scott and Bonna Brooks

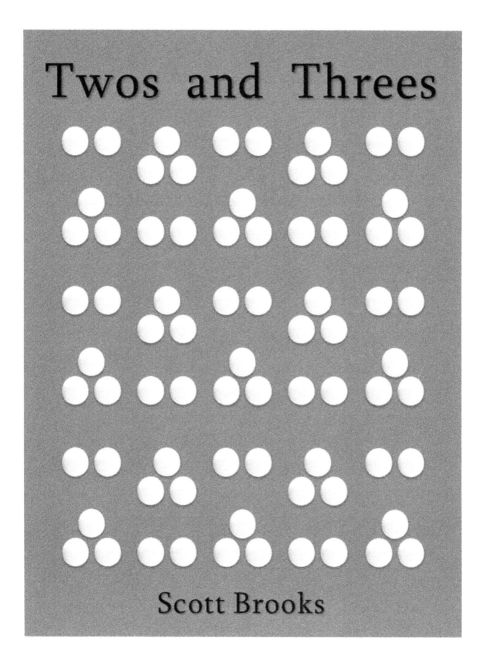

Twos and Threes

By Scott Brooks

Available at www.BrooksFamilyStore.com

ISBN 978-1-4835525-5-2

Table of Contents for Book 1 – *Twos and Threes*

Dedication

I dedicate this book to you the reader – especially if you have longed for better fellowship but have not been able to find it. May Jesus use this book and work in your life to bring you to wonderful friendships of true heart-to-heart fellowship!

Chapter 1 – Introduction

I am really excited about this book! For years I have had a deep heart's desire to see Christians truly experience wonderful fellowship and through it to grow in wonderful friendships both with the Lord and each other. But my dilemma was that I never knew how to clearly communicate things that would help us all to experience true heart-to-heart fellowship in a greater way. That is until recently when Jesus helped me to understand what I had been missing, which I will state in the following claim:

> **It is of great value for each of us to have the freedom to count twos and threes fellowship as more significant than things that are one to many.**

In the rest of this book I will share with you the reasons for this claim. As you read, I hope the Holy Spirit encourages you and uses this book material to establish an anchor of freedom for you to enjoy and be encouraged by 2s-and-3s fellowship all the more.

Since 2s-and-3s may work a little differently in your life than they have in mine, please feel free to join me in the following prayer so that Jesus can uniquely tailor this book to each of our lives.

> Dear Jesus,
>
> As I read this book, please teach me through it and make things stand out to me that are Your best for my life. And over time, please help me to keep hold of these things by Your grace and enabling.
>
> In Jesus' name,
>
> Your Name

Before continuing, I would first like to note where this book fits in the sequence of books that the Lord has had us write. I say "us" instead of "me" since my wife, Bonna, was the co-author of the first book listed below:

      1. Would you like to see an Amazing Miracle? (Free at www. SeeMiracle.com)

      2. Deeper Friendships (Free at www.DeeperFriendships.com)

      3. At His Feet (At www.OrderAtHisFeet.com)

      4. Twos and Threes (At www.BrooksFamilyStore.com)

The first three books build a foundation for this ***Twos and Threes*** book. Although this is the case, ***Twos and Threes*** is written standalone enough so that you can read it without having to first read the other three books. So, if you have not read the first three books, you may still want to do so after reading this book so as to get a fuller explanation of those foundational concepts.

With all of this now said, I hope Jesus richly blesses you through this book!

Chapter 2 – How Twos and Threes works

> For where **two or three** gather in my name, there am I with
> them. (Matthew 18:20, emphasis mine)

In this verse, Jesus states the main building block of Christian
fellowship and friendships – which is when two or three gather in His
name.

In various 1-to-many settings this verse is often misquoted by the 1
to say "two or more" instead of its correct form of "two or three". We
will explore the reason for this misquote in the next chapter where
we will look at the historic shift that caused the 1-to-many model to
often upstage the primary focus upon 2s-and-3s. But in this chapter
we will explore how 2s-and-3s fellowship works – including why it is
so incredibly valuable and what Jesus is wonderfully bringing about
through it!

Overall, Jesus has designed 2s-and-3s to be an integral and
significant part of His **freeing** each of us to function as He has created
us to function – which is for each of us to have wonderful friendships
of agape love with Him and each other.

> So if the Son sets you **free**, you will be **free** indeed. (John
> 8:36, emphasis mine)

> One of the teachers of the law came and heard them debating.
> Noticing that Jesus had given them a good answer, he asked
> him, "Of all the commandments, which is the most important?"
> "The most important one," answered Jesus, "is this: 'Hear, O
> Israel: The Lord our God, the Lord is one. **Love the Lord your
> God with all your heart and with all your soul and with all
> your mind and with all your strength.**' The second is this:
> '**Love your neighbor as yourself.**' There is no commandment
> greater than these." (Mark 12:28-31, emphasis mine)

> I (Jesus) no longer call you servants, because a servant does not know his master's business. Instead, I have called you **friends**, for everything that I learned from my Father I have made known to you. (John 15:15, emphasis mine)

So, how does Jesus use 2s-and-3s in this process?

The following four steps show how this works. These steps use a group of 3 as an example, with you being 1 of the 3. The same would hold true if it was a group of 2 instead of 3.

Step 1: Jesus works continually in you through His Holy Spirit to both filter and enhance the data coming into you via your senses by giving you a sense of what is best for you to reject, and to give you insights into those things that are best for you to receive.

> But when he, the (Holy) Spirit of truth, comes, he will guide you into all the truth. (John 16:13a)

For example, when you hear someone speaking you may sense that something is not quite right in what they are saying and therefore it is best to not receive it – hence filtering the data coming into you. Or when someone shares something with you, something might stand out to you as the Holy Spirit gives you insights into it – hence the enhancing of the data coming into you.

Step 2: As you meet with two others, you are now in a 2s-and-3s. The Holy Spirit will work in your mind and heart, and will help you to share your heart with the other two people.

Step 3: As the other two people listen to you share, the Holy Spirit will work in both of them to filter and enhance what you have shared with them so as to uniquely tailor it to each of their lives.

Step 4: The ball of fellowship rolls along as the Holy Spirit helps each person to share their heart with the other two, and the Holy Spirit also filters and enhances the data going into each person.

Overall, if this 4-step process is working well, each person will be encouraged through the 2s-and-3s fellowship, and their friendships with each other will grow. And as each person grows in friendship qualities, it will in turn help them to grow in their friendship with Jesus – which is by far the greatest thing in life on earth and throughout eternity!

There are many additional benefits of 2s-and-3s fellowship – some that I know about and some that I do not know about. The reason for this is because the Lord is incredibly smarter than we can possibly know or imagine, and He is the Creator of life on earth. As such, Jesus has designed things in a way so that they tie to the two greatest commandments to love God and to love our neighbors as ourselves. And He uses 2s-and-3s fellowship as a key part of this. With this now said, throughout the rest of this chapter we will explore some additional benefits of 2s-and-3s fellowship that I currently know about. And over time may Jesus help us all to learn even more benefits – since He is the One who knows all of them!

The following are a few benefits I am currently aware of:

~ Growing in knowledge

~ Mutual encouragement

~ Strengthening against sin

~ Spiritual growth

Please note that these are not mutually exclusive categories since many of the items within each category also apply to other categories as well. For example, there are things in **Mutual Encouragement** that also apply to **Strengthening against sin**. So, you might categorize these in different ways than I have, but hopefully the above categories will give us a good place to start.

We will now look at each of these categories in greater detail.

Growing in Knowledge

In the 4-step process we looked at earlier, the Holy Spirit was mentioned in each step since He is the biggest key to 2s-and-3s fellowship working well!

The Holy Spirit helps each person with what words they share and also in filtering and enhancing what the others hear. This allows Him to work through 2s-and-3s to grow each of us in knowledge and a greater understanding of truth.

> But when he, **the (Holy) Spirit of truth**, comes, **he will guide you into all the truth**. (John 16:13a, emphasis mine)

The Holy Spirit could impart this knowledge directly to each of us – as He sometimes does through what we read in the Bible, dreams, and other means. But the Holy Spirit works through 2s-and-3s to grow each person in knowledge by their hearing the knowledge that He has grown the others in, and then He also helps each person to know how that knowledge specifically applies to their life.

An example of this has occurred during the many times where I had been learning a lesson from the Lord, and as I shared with one or two other Christians, I was quite surprised that they had been going through a similar lesson. As we shared back and forth, the combined knowledge helped each of us to gain a greater understanding. The Holy Spirit used and continues to use this process to help each of us to grow in excellent ways.

> Instead, **speaking the truth in love, we will grow to become in every respect the mature** body of him who is the head, that is, Christ. (Ephesians 4:15, emphasis mine)

Through the 2s-and-3s we also grow in knowledge of each other. The Lord uses this to help us to appreciate each other more, enjoy each other more, understand how to pray for and help each other, how to be sensitive to each other, and so much more.

Through the 2s-and-3s we also grow in appreciation of Jesus. For example, if you and I are in a 2s-and-3s and we decide to look at the following well known scripture:

> For God so loved the world that he gave his one and only Son, that whoever believes in him shall not perish but have eternal life. (John 3:16)

And then we share with each other what stands out to us. You might share how you were touched by how much Jesus loves us to do something so wonderful for not only you, but for all humans too! And I might share with you how thankful I am to know that the Lord is willing to preserve our existence forever! And through this 2s-and-3s sharing, both of us wind up appreciating all the more how wonderful Jesus is!

Mutual Encouragement

When Jesus sent out the seventy-two disciples, He did not send each of them out separately. Instead He sent them out by 2s.

> After this the Lord appointed seventy-two others and **sent them two by two** ahead of him to every town and place where he was about to go. (Luke 10:1, emphasis mine)

In a similar way, people often use the "buddy system" and prefer going to places with a friend rather than going by themselves. Not only can it make them feel safer, but they can also be encouraged by each other's company. And being with another person can also help against the loneliness that so many people struggle with.

In the book of Acts, we see numerous examples of teams of two or three, such as Peter + John, Paul + Barnabas, Paul + Silas, and Priscilla + Aquila + Apollos. And as they faced difficult situations together, they were encouraged by each other. For example, in Acts 16 we see that Paul and Silas went through a very difficult time.

> The crowd joined in the attack against Paul and Silas, and the magistrates ordered them to be stripped and beaten with rods. After they had been severely flogged, they were thrown into prison, and the jailer was commanded to guard them carefully. When he received these orders, he put them in the inner cell and fastened their feet in the stocks. (Acts 16:22-24)

I think there is a good possibility that both of them were discouraged by the rejection, flogging, imprisonment, and having their feet fastened in stocks. But amazingly, somehow the Lord strengthened them and they found mutual encouragement as is seen in the next verse.

> About midnight Paul and Silas were praying and singing hymns to God, and the other prisoners were listening to them. (Acts 16:25)

And in the book of Luke, it tells about two disciples who were walking to Emmaus after Jesus had been crucified. They were both struggling with Jesus having been executed even though they had hoped He was going to redeem Israel.

> Now that same day two of them were going to a village called Emmaus, about seven miles from Jerusalem. **They were talking with each other about everything that had happened.** As they talked and discussed these things with each other, Jesus himself came up and walked along with them; but they were kept from recognizing him. He asked them, "What are you discussing together as you walk along?" **They stood still, their faces downcast.** One of them, named Cleopas, asked him, "Are you the only one visiting Jerusalem who does not know the things that have happened there

in these days?" "What things?" he asked. "About Jesus of Nazareth," they replied. "He was a prophet, powerful in word and deed before God and all the people. **The chief priests and our rulers handed him over to be sentenced to death, and they crucified him; but we had hoped that he was the one who was going to redeem Israel.** And what is more, it is the third day since all this took place. (Luke 24:13-21, emphasis mine)

As Jesus shared with them in a group of 3, they both were so encouraged that they got up and traveled about seven miles to share with others their excitement about Jesus having been resurrected and now being alive!

They got up and returned at once to Jerusalem. There they found the Eleven and those with them, assembled together and saying, "It is true! The Lord has risen and has appeared to Simon." Then the two told what had happened on the way, and how Jesus was recognized by them when he broke the bread. (Luke 24:33-35)

So they experienced an event, and afterwards they compared notes with each other. Some people call this a meeting-after-the-meeting, where each person shares what they had experienced, and through this combined knowledge, everyone can gain a better perspective. And through this sharing, everyone can be mutually encouraged as well.

There are many additional reasons why I find 2s-and-3s fellowship to be very encouraging, but I am not sure all the reasons why. It is like saying, "Why do I like rainbows, sunsets, and waterfalls?" I can attempt to explain why, but I would still feel like there are reasons that I do not fully understand. I think part of the reason for this is because Jesus is incredibly smart and has designed us in such a way that we tend to like certain things – such as breathing air and enjoying rainbows. In other words, it is who we are. In a similar way, I find many things that are encouraging about good heart-to-heart 2s-and-3s fellowship. The following are some of those things. My guess is that if you came up with your own list, it would be similar to mine, and yet have things listed that would be according to how Jesus has uniquely made and tuned you. So, here are some additional things that I find encouraging about good 2s-and-3s fellowship…

Many people struggle with loneliness. I find that 2s-and-3s can help to alleviate loneliness by helping each person to feel relationally connected rather than relationally isolated.

Friendships can develop well in 2s-and-3s. And I find it encouraging to have friends and to enjoy friends – especially in times of 2s-and-3s fellowship.

I have often been encouraged to find missing pieces of insights that have been eluding me as the Holy Spirit brings in insights through 2s-and-3s – both through what others share and also what the Holy Spirit makes alive to me.

I often find it encouraging to have someone pray for me in 2s-and-3s.

> He has delivered us from such a deadly peril, and he will deliver us again. On him we have set our hope that he will continue to deliver us, **as you help us by your prayers. Then many will give thanks on our behalf for the gracious favor granted us in answer to the prayers of many.** (2 Corinthians 1:10-11, emphasis mine)

I find it encouraging to simply enjoy the company of others in 2s-and-3s.

I find it encouraging to see others encouraged as Jesus works through 2s-and-3s fellowship.

As someone shares what they have been going through and it turns out to be similar to what I have been going through, then I find it encouraging to know that I am not the only one going through it.

If I am troubled and my emotions are stirred, I sometimes find it encouraging sharing with others in 2s-and-3s. As we share back and forth, it is often like a log jam on a river being broken up so that the logs can once again flow down the river – in other words, we can feel freed up in our hearts. So I find it encouraging when others are a sounding board for me and also encouraging when I can be a sounding board for them. As we listen well to each other and then share accordingly, we are often mutually encouraged.

Sometimes I find it challenging to keep a good perspective on life. And when I hear others share in 2s-and-3s, I am often encouraged by hearing their perspective. For example, if I am feeling like I have been going through more trials than usual, and the other person shares about how excited they are to eventually be in Heaven with Jesus forever, then I can be encouraged by realizing that indeed our light and momentary trials are not worth comparing to what will be eternal!

> I consider that our present sufferings **are not worth comparing** with the glory that will be revealed in us. (Romans 8:18, emphasis mine)

With how conducive 2s-and-3s are for people sharing their hearts with each other, I find it encouraging just hearing others share at a heart level.

As others share truthfully, I often find it freeing to me.

> To the Jews who had believed him, Jesus said, "If you hold to my teaching, you are really my disciples. **Then you will know the truth, and the truth will set you free.**" (John 8:31-32, emphasis mine)

For example, if someone shares how they have been blessed lately by Romans 8:28:

> And we know that in all things God works for the good of those who love him, who have been called according to his purpose. (Romans 8:28)

Then I may in turn be encouraged by this truth, as I am all the more thankful that God is working for good in my life as well.

In 2s-and-3s fellowship I find it encouraging when I sometimes sense the Lord's presence in a greater way.

> For where two or three gather in my (Jesus') name, **there am I with them**. (Matthew 18:20, emphasis mine)

I find it encouraging to be better understood by others and to understand others better. I find 2s-and-3s fellowship to often be very helpful in this process.

I find 2s-and-3s to be encouraging when it helps me to appreciate Jesus, others, and even myself better. So, if someone shares something they appreciate about Jesus, it often helps me to appreciate Jesus all the more and I am encouraged that He truly is the way that He is. And if someone shares what they appreciate about someone else, then it can help me to better appreciate that person as well, and I can be encouraged that they are indeed that way. And I often find it encouraging when others share something they appreciate about me, and it can help me to appreciate what the Lord has been doing in my life.

If I am a bit weighed down by life, I find that laughing together with others in 2s-and-3s is often very encouraging.

If I see Jesus' love in the eyes of others, then I find it to be very encouraging! It can also help me to realize His love for me in a greater way!

Strengthening against sin

In the last section we looked at many ways that 2s-and-3s fellowship is mutually encouraging. One of the benefits that we did not look at is how mutual encouragement can help us to avoid sin. The following verses show this correlation.

> See to it, brothers and sisters, that none of you has a sinful, unbelieving heart that turns away from the living God. But **encourage one another daily**, as long as it is called "Today," **so that none of you may be hardened by sin's deceitfulness**. (Hebrews 3:12-13, emphasis mine)

So the question is, "How can the daily mutual encouragement of 2s-and-3s fellowship help us to not be hardened by sin's deceitfulness?"

There may be many reasons for this, but here is one that I am aware of…

Sin is deceitful in that it claims to give something positive that it will not actually provide. It is also deceitful in trying to hide what the true negative consequences will be. For example, when Eve was tempted by satan (who was possessing a serpent), she thought she would gain her perceived benefit of enjoying the fruit, gaining wisdom, and becoming more like God in knowing good and evil.

> Now the serpent was more crafty than any of the wild animals the Lord God had made. He said to the woman, "Did God really say, 'You must not eat from any tree in the garden'?" The woman said to the serpent, "We may eat fruit from the trees in the garden, but God did say, 'You must not eat fruit from the tree that is in the middle of the garden, and you must not touch it, or you will die.'" "You will not certainly die," the serpent said to the woman. "For God knows that when you eat from it your eyes will be opened, and you will be like God,

knowing good and evil." When the woman saw that the fruit of
the tree was good for food and pleasing to the eye, and also
desirable for gaining wisdom, she took some and ate it. She
also gave some to her husband, who was with her, and he ate
it. (Genesis 3:1-6)

But Eve did not realize that the picture in her mind of what she
thought would happen was indeed very different from the reality of
all the negative effects that would result. This includes not only the
negative effects she would experience – such as getting removed
from the Garden of Eden, having pains in childbirth, and having her
one son murder her other son – but also all the negative effects that
would occur to the whole world, such as war, famine, murder, and so
much more!

If Eve had someone to have 2s-and-3s fellowship with, whom at
a prior time had followed the serpent's advice and had terrible
outcomes, and that person shared with her what they went through,
then it may have encouraged Eve to not take the terrible step into sin
that she did.

If we look at this in the context of the entire Bible, we see that the
essence of sin is the relational violations that occur against the two
greatest commandments – for each of us to love God and to love
our neighbors as ourselves. The demons hate God and therefore
are always working against us by trying to keep us from being able
to love God and those God has created – including ourselves. So,
the demons wrap even good things into a sinful package, so that if
we take the package, we will wind up pulling our hearts away from
God and even hardening our hearts against God in the process. This
in turn will hinder the fruit of God's Holy Spirit from flowing through
us. Since the first fruit of the Holy Spirit listed is agape love, then our
relationships will be devoid of God's love. So, instead of having God's
love flowing in our relationships, there will often be at least some
hatred.

> At one time we too were foolish, disobedient, deceived and enslaved by all kinds of passions and pleasures. We lived in malice and envy, **being hated and hating one another**. (Titus 3:3, emphasis mine)

I am glad Jesus works through 2s-and-3s fellowship to help us to be mutually encouraged so that by His grace we can better avoid the deceitfulness of sin and its terrible effects upon relationships.

Spiritual Growth

In Jesus' tremendous love for us, He works in incredible detail to help each of us to grow spiritually for our good. My brain is not big enough to begin to map out how Jesus is doing this in my life, let alone to understand how He is doing this in the lives of others as well. Jesus is definitely the only One smart enough to be the pioneer and perfecter of our faith!

> Therefore, since we are surrounded by such a great cloud of witnesses, let us throw off everything that hinders and the sin that so easily entangles. And let us run with perseverance the race marked out for us, fixing our eyes on **Jesus, the pioneer and perfecter of faith**. For the joy set before him he endured the cross, scorning its shame, and sat down at the right hand of the throne of God. (Hebrews 12:1-2, emphasis mine)

And Jesus uses 2s-and-3s as a key part of this spiritual growth process!

In the parable of the seeds, Jesus shared how different plants grew well when they were planted in good soil.

> Still other seed fell on good soil, where it produced a crop—a hundred, sixty or thirty times what was sown. (Matthew 13:8)

The good soil was the only soil condition where the seeds grew well. And a growing seed is metaphorical to a person growing well spiritually.

> But **the seed falling on good soil refers to someone who hears the word and understands it. This is the one who produces a crop**, yielding a hundred, sixty or thirty times what was sown. (Matthew 13:23, emphasis mine)

2s-and-3s fellowship is a key part of this spiritual growth process in that it helps our heart soil to be able to receive the seed as the Holy Spirit works through the entire 4-step process. For example, we can clearly see this in step 3.

> **Step 3:** As the other two people listen to you share, the Holy Spirit will work in both of them to filter and enhance what you have shared with them so as to uniquely tailor it to each of their lives.

If the hearts of the people are not responsive to the Holy Spirit then it will greatly hinder this process. In the middle of the parable of the seeds, Jesus shared the following:

> In them is fulfilled the prophecy of Isaiah: "'You will be ever hearing but never understanding; you will be ever seeing but never perceiving. For this people's heart has become calloused; they hardly hear with their ears, and they have closed their eyes. Otherwise they might see with their eyes, hear with their ears, understand with their hearts and turn, and I would heal them.' But blessed are your eyes because they see, and your ears because they hear. For truly I tell you, many prophets and righteous people longed to see what you see but did not see it, and to hear what you hear but did not hear it. (Matthew 13:14-17)

So, good 2s-and-3s fellowship greatly helps us to have good heart soil so that we can grow well spiritually.

> See to it, brothers and sisters, that none of you has a sinful, unbelieving heart that turns away from the living God. But **encourage one another daily**, as long as it is called "Today," **so that none of you may be hardened by sin's deceitfulness**. (Hebrews 3:12-13, emphasis mine)

Stated another way in terms of spiritual sharpness, without good 2s-and-3s fellowship we are more likely to become spiritually dull like Jesus' disciples who were not able to understand the meaning of a parable Jesus had just shared with them.

> Peter said, "Explain the parable to us." "**Are you still so dull?**" Jesus asked them. "**Don't you see** that…" (Matthew 15:15-17a, emphasis mine)

Instead, the Holy Spirit works through good 2s-and-3s fellowship to spiritually sharpen us so that we can learn well from the Lord.

> As iron **sharpens** iron, so one person **sharpens** another. (Proverbs 27:17, emphasis mine)

The bottom line of all of this is that Jesus uses 2s-and-3s fellowship as a big key for each of us to grow toward spiritual maturity.

> Instead, **speaking the truth in love, we will grow to become in every respect the mature** body of him who is the head, that is, Christ. (Ephesians 4:15, emphasis mine)

It would be nice to hear your thoughts

I hope you were encouraged reading about some of the benefits of good 2s-and-3s fellowship. I would now love to hear you share your heart as to the reasons why you value 2s-and-3s fellowship. But unfortunately, in book writing I lose out on getting to hear your thoughts. It reminds me of the verse where John said:

I have much to write to you, but **I do not want to use paper and ink. Instead, I hope to visit you and talk with you face to face**, so that our joy may be complete. (2 John 1:12, emphasis mine)

Summary

In this chapter we looked at how the Holy Spirit works through a 4-step process to bring about wonderful things in 2s-and-3s fellowship! I hope the Holy Spirit encouraged you as you read through some of the many benefits of 2s-and-3s fellowship.

In the next chapter we will look at the historic shift toward 1-to-many settings that has often worked against people participating in and greatly benefiting from 2s-and-3s fellowship.

Chapter 3 – The Historic Shift

I have blue eyes that tend to be a little bit more sensitive to glare than they would possibly be if they were a darker color, such as brown. I am not totally sure if this is the case, but I do notice that I tend to be more affected by glare than people who have darker eyes. And when I drive a car it is even worse, since the front windshield adds to the glare. So, I usually wear sunglasses when I drive a car in the daytime. And I have tried different tinted lenses over time to see what tint works best against glare. I have tried lighter and darker tints of yellow, blue, and green. As part of this process, I have found that the tint of the sunglasses makes the world appear differently to me. Overall, I tend to like a slightly darker shade of green since it seems to change the tints the least for me – for example, green trees and grass still look green and it also does not seem to affect the look of the blue sky too much.

In a similar way, a shift began to occur at the time of Roman Emperor Constantine that eventually resulted in a 1-to-many pattern getting established. And this 1-to-many pattern has been around for so long that people tend to look at things through the tinted lens of this pattern – including in what they see in the Bible. If on the other hand, they started only with the Bible and looked at what the Bible says, then they would see a very different picture as to how things truly looked in Biblical times before the 1-to-many pattern became established. To say this another way, the 1-to-many pattern has been around for such a long time that people tend to think it is the way it has always been, when in reality things originally looked quite different from it.

So, in this chapter we will look at this historic shift by first looking at how things were before the time of Constantine. We will then look at how things have changed during the time of Constantine and up to the current date. And in this we will look at the negative impact this shift has had upon 2s-and-3s fellowship.

How it originally looked

The New Testament paints a picture of houses being one of the predominant places where Christians gathered. We can see this in the following verses that use the English term "church" instead of the original Greek word "ekklesia" which means an assembly of people.

> Greet also **the church that meets at their house**. (Romans 16:5a, emphasis mine)

> Aquila and Priscilla greet you warmly in the Lord, and so does **the church that meets at their house**. (1 Corinthians 16:19b, emphasis mine)

> Give my greetings to the brothers and sisters at Laodicea, and to Nympha and **the church in her house**. (Colossians 4:15, emphasis mine)

> also to Apphia our sister and Archippus our fellow soldier— and to **the church that meets in your home**: (Philemon 1:2, emphasis mine)

And as these Christians gathered together in houses, they shared meals together, had communion together (breaking of bread), prayed together, shared their hearts with each other, and encouraged each other.

> **They broke bread in their homes and ate together** with glad and sincere hearts, (Acts 2:46b, emphasis mine)

> After Paul and Silas came out of the prison, they went to **Lydia's house, where they met with the brothers and sisters and encouraged them**. Then they left. (Acts 16:40, emphasis mine)

> When this had dawned on him, he **went to the house of Mary**

the mother of John, also called Mark, **where many people had gathered and were praying**. (Acts 12:12, emphasis mine)

So, we see a picture of people gathering together, enjoying friendships with each other, and building each other up in mutual encouragement. This looks a lot like the Last Supper where Jesus shared a meal with His disciples and we can see 2s-and-3s at work when Peter asked John to ask Jesus the question of who would betray Jesus.

> After he had said this, Jesus was troubled in spirit and testified, "Very truly I tell you, one of you is going to betray me." His disciples stared at one another, at a loss to know which of them he meant. **One of them (John), the disciple whom Jesus loved, was reclining next to him. Simon Peter motioned to this disciple and said, "Ask him which one he means." Leaning back against Jesus, he asked him, "Lord, who is it?"** (John 13:21-25, emphasis mine)

So even though there were more than three people gathered for a meal, we can see that there can be groupings of 2s-and-3s within a larger group, which often happens when a group of people share a meal at a table.

And we can also see from the following verses that this encouraging fellowship was not isolated to a single day of the week but was interwoven into the daily lives of the Christians.

> See to it, brothers and sisters, that none of you has a sinful, unbelieving heart that turns away from the living God. But **encourage one another daily**, as long as it is called "Today," so that none of you may be hardened by sin's deceitfulness. (Hebrews 3:12-13, emphasis mine)

The shift toward 1-to-many

Roman Emperor Constantine lived from the year 272 to the year 337. He was the first Roman Emperor to become a Christian. Even though some people question the validity of his conversion, he did implement reforms favorable to Christians – such as his initiating the Edict of Milan which gave Christians the right to worship the Lord. This added safety allowed Christians to become more public without the threat of losing their lives as was the case in the time of some of the prior Emperors – such as Nero who cruelly burned Christians to death as torches to provide evening light.

This overall shift eventually led the way to Roman Emperor Theodosius 1 putting forth decrees that resulted in Christianity becoming the state religion of the Roman Empire in the year 380 – hence the Roman Catholic Church becomes the state religion.

For the most part, it was advantageous for Roman citizens to become members of this Roman Catholic Church. This led to both Christians and non-Christians joining the Church. Most of these people were illiterate. So to educate the people, the Mass was partly established as a teaching tool. And in this, a priest would step the congregation through the Mass.

Through all of this, a 1-to-many pattern became established with the priest being the 1 leading the many in the Mass. In one way, it makes sense since they wanted to educate illiterate people. But what may not have been apparent at the time was the effect it would have upon 2s-and-3s, since the 1-to-many pattern became the primary focus instead of 2s-and-3s.

This 1-to-many Roman Catholic pattern has existed all the way up to this present day.

Protestantism

A Roman Catholic priest named Martin Luther lived from the year 1483 to the year 1546. Martin wrote down ninety-five things about the Roman Catholic Church that he thought should be changed. And in the year 1517 he posted this list on the door of the Catholic Church in Wittenberg, Germany. Eventually this escalated into such a conflict that a church split occurred, with Martin Luther going in a different direction from the Catholic Church by his forming one of the first Protestant Churches – which eventually became known as the Lutheran Church.

This Protestant Church was very similar to the Catholic Church in that it still maintained a 1-to-many pattern. In other words, Martin did make a number of changes, but none of these changes affected it still being a 1-to-many pattern. For example, Martin wrote his own German Mass which was a modified version of the Catholic Mass that the 1 would lead the many through. And extra focus was given to the sermon time as the means for the 1 to educate the many.

This 1-to-many Protestant pattern has existed all the way up to this present day.

Multiple Flavors

Over the years there have been many forms of Catholic and Protestant churches. But for the most part, these patterns tend to still be 1-to-many centric instead of having a primary focus upon 2s-and-3s.

Self-Reinforcing Preservation

There are many things that are done for the preservation of an organization. This makes sense since if an organization cannot preserve its existence, then it cannot provide the goods and services that it does. And if it ceases to exist, then it also cannot benefit from the things that it does – such as being able to pay its employees. So, sales ads try to reinforce how wonderful a company is and why people should buy the products produced by that company.

One thing that may be hard to accept is that the same holds true for the 1-to-many Catholic and Protestant organizations. Certain things have been done over time for the preservation of these organizations. One might think that all of these things would be altruistic, but in reality, even if there have been many altruistic reasons, there have also been reasons that are at least misleading and possibly even dishonest, that have worked to shift the focus from 2s-and-3s to 1-to-many. There may be many areas where this has occurred, but there are two areas I am aware of that have clearly contributed to this shift of focus. The one is the use of Bible verses out of context, and the other is in regard to what people know as "sacraments" such as baptism and communion.

Bible verses out of context

In the second chapter of this book, I wrote:

> For where **two or three** gather in my name, there am I with them. (Matthew 18:20, emphasis mine)

> In this verse, Jesus states the main building block of Christian fellowship and friendships – which is when two or three gather in His name.

> In various 1-to-many settings this verse is often misquoted by the 1 to say "two or more" instead of its correct form of "two or three". We will explore the reason for this misquote in the next chapter where we will look at the historic shift that caused the 1-to-many model to often upstage the primary focus upon 2s-and-3s.

In light of what you have already read in this Historic Shift chapter,

I hope it is now clear why this verse is often misquoted as "two or more" instead of its correct form of "two or three", since "two or more" supports 1-to-many organizations better than the correct reading of "two or three".

And people are often told, "Do not forsake the gathering" to mean that they need to go to a 1-to-many setting on a Sunday morning. Once again, the person saying "Do not forsake the gathering" may have altruistic motives in wanting good things for the person they are saying this to – since they may think it would be best for the person to join them in the 1-to-many setting they belong to. But the person saying this may not even realize this verse has been shared with them from the pulpit – but out of its true Biblical context.

If we look at this verse in the entire context of Hebrews 10, we see that it is encouraging Christians to gather together for mutual encouragement to help them to avoid deliberate sin.

> Therefore, brothers and sisters, since we have confidence to enter the Most Holy Place by the blood of Jesus, by a new and living way opened for us through the curtain, that is, his body, and since we have a great priest (Jesus) over the house of God, let us draw near to God with a sincere heart and with the full assurance that faith brings, having our hearts sprinkled to cleanse us from a guilty conscience and having our bodies washed with pure water. Let us hold unswervingly to the hope we profess, for he who promised is faithful. **And let us consider how we may spur one another on toward love and good deeds, not giving up meeting together, as some are in the habit of doing, but encouraging one another— and all the more as you see the Day approaching. If we deliberately keep on sinning after we have received the knowledge of the truth, no sacrifice for sins is left, but only a fearful expectation of judgment** and of raging fire that will consume the enemies of God. (Hebrews 10:19-27, emphasis mine)

And Hebrews 10 directly parallels Hebrews 3 which shows that this mutual encouragement is to be more than weekly – in other words, not limited to a Sunday morning.

> So, as the Holy Spirit says: "Today, if you hear his voice, do not harden your hearts as you did in the rebellion, during the time of testing in the wilderness, where your ancestors tested and tried me, though for forty years they saw what I did. That is why I was angry with that generation; I said, 'Their hearts are always going astray, and they have not known my ways.' So I declared on oath in my anger, 'They shall never enter my rest.' " See to it, brothers and sisters, that none of you has a sinful, unbelieving heart that turns away from the living God. **But encourage one another daily**, as long as it is called "Today," **so that none of you may be hardened by sin's deceitfulness**. We have come to share in Christ, if indeed we hold our original conviction firmly to the very end. (Hebrews 3:7-14, emphasis mine)

And from the last chapter we saw how 2s-and-3s is very conducive to this needed mutual encouragement since all four steps of the 4-step process are included. In contrast, this "mutual" part tends to be missing in 1-to-many settings since they focus only on a small part of the 4-step process. As such, the 1-to-many settings do not work as well as 2s-and-3s for providing this daily mutual encouragement.

Another saying which is often said by the 1 is not even a Bible verse. The 1 says, "Come to be fed". It is the concept of the many attending a 1-to-many gathering to be fed teachings from the 1 – like sheep being fed by a shepherd. It is also taught that without this feeding, that the many will go astray like lost sheep. Once again the focus is upon 1-to-many instead of the 2s-and-3s that is so helpful against the deceitfulness of sin and in turn against people going astray from the Lord.

This is similar to the common question of, "Who is your covering?"

This question implies that you need to be covered by the 1 in a 1-to-many setting in order to stay on track with the Lord. But again, this is not a Biblical quote even though the people asking this question often make it sound as if it is.

These are but a few of the examples that help to ensure the existence of these 1-to-many organizations. It may even come from good motives, but using these Bible verses and sayings out of Biblical context can once again work to undermine valuable 2s-and-3s fellowship.

Sacraments

Another way that the 1-to-many Catholic and Protestant churches have been self-preserving is by gathering up what they refer to as "sacraments" so that the sacraments can only be performed by the 1 or others appointed by the 1. This includes such sacraments as baptism and communion.

From a logical standpoint, if only these two organizations can perform such sacraments, then does it mean that before these organizations came into existence that Christians in New Testament times were not able to be baptized and take communion, and in turn be forgiven of their sins?

The answer of course is No.

Instead, when New Testament Christians met in homes, they had communion as part of their meals together. And any Christian could baptize others.

And as for the forgiveness of sins, it is Biblically tied to the personal action of a person repenting (turning from sin), confessing their sin (coming into agreement with God about it), and asking God to forgive them according to His payment for them on the Cross.

So, even 1 John 1:9 is taken out of its context and placed into liturgy so that the 1 can declare the forgiveness of sins to the many whether or not all of the many are actually Christians. But if we look at the true Biblical context of this verse, we can see that it is about the restoration of fellowship – which once again is more conducive in 2s-and-3s.

Here is 1 John 1:9 all by itself without the rest of the chapter:

> If we confess our sins, he is faithful and just and will forgive us our sins and purify us from all unrighteousness. (1 John 1:9)

And here is 1 John 1:9 in the context of the entire first chapter of 1 John:

> That which was from the beginning, which we have heard, which we have seen with our eyes, which we have looked at and our hands have touched—this we proclaim concerning the Word of life (Jesus). The life appeared; we have seen it and testify to it, and we proclaim to you the eternal life, which was with the Father and has appeared to us. **We proclaim to you what we have seen and heard, so that you also may have fellowship with us. And our fellowship is with the Father and with his Son, Jesus Christ.** We write this to make our joy complete. This is the message we have heard from him and declare to you: God is light; in him there is no darkness at all. **If we claim to have fellowship with him** and yet walk in the darkness, we lie and do not live out the truth. **But if we walk in the light, as he is in the light, we have fellowship with one another, and the blood of Jesus, his Son, purifies us from all sin.** If we claim to be without sin, we deceive ourselves and the truth is not in us. **If we confess our sins, he is faithful and just and will forgive us our sins and purify us from all unrighteousness.** If we claim we have not sinned, we make him out to be a liar and his word is not in us. (1 John 1:1-10, emphasis mine)

So, many people think that the 1-to-many weekly setting of a Catholic or Protestant church is needed for them to partake of these sacraments, but if they instead first look through the lens of starting with what the Bible says, they will find that it is truly not the case. Instead, if they are a Christian, then they can personally partake of such sacraments outside of the 1-to-many settings.

Summary

In this chapter we looked at the historic shift that started in the time of Roman Emperor Constantine that caused the main building block of 2s-and-3s to often be replaced with a 1-to-many focus. Instead of meeting in houses and sharing meals together, as they did in Biblical times where 2s-and-3s fellowship thrived, the emergence of the Catholic and Protestant church forms brought with it a shift where the primary focus moved away from 2s-and-3s to instead be replaced with various forms of 1-to-many.

In the next chapter we will look at some confirming observations as to why this shift toward the 1-to-many has worked against people attaining the great benefits of 2s-and-3s.

ENDNOTES

Constantine the Great
http://en.wikipedia.org/wiki/Constantine_the_Great
Site accessed 12/11/2014

The Emperor's New Religion, The story of early Christianity's most famous-and most controversial-convert by Bruce Shelley posted 1/01/1998 12:00AM.
http://www.christianitytoday.com/ch/1998/issue57/57h038.html?start=1
Site accessed 11/5/2014

From the Archives: Nero's Cruelties An account from Roman historian
Tacitus (C. 115)　posted 6/30/2008 12:36PM
http://www.christianitytoday.com/ch/1990/issue27/
fromthearchivesneroscruelties.html
Site accessed 11/5/2014

State church of the Roman Empire
http://en.wikipedia.org/wiki/State_church_of_the_Roman_Empire
Site accessed 12/13/2014

Edict of Thessalonica
http://en.wikipedia.org/wiki/Edict_of_Thessalonica
Site accessed 12/13/2014

Decline of Greco-Roman polytheism
http://en.wikipedia.org/wiki/Decline_of_Greco-Roman_polytheism
Site accessed 12/16/2014

User:Cynwolfe/literacy and education in the Roman Empire
http://en.wikipedia.org/wiki/User:Cynwolfe/literacy_and_education_in_
the_Roman_Empire
Site accessed 11/7/2014

Christianity in the 1st century
http://en.wikipedia.org/wiki/Christianity_in_the_1st_century
Site accessed 12/16/2014

Catholic Encyclopedia (1913)/Liturgy of the Mass
http://en.wikisource.org/wiki/Catholic_Encyclopedia_(1913)/Liturgy_
of_the_Mass
Site accessed 12/16/2014

Mass (liturgy)
http://en.wikipedia.org/wiki/Mass_(liturgy)
Site accessed 12/16/2014

Catholic Church
http://en.wikipedia.org/wiki/Catholic_Church
Site accessed 12/13/2014

Catholicism
http://en.wikipedia.org/wiki/Catholicism
Site accessed 12/13/2014

Martin Luther
http://en.wikipedia.org/wiki/Martin_Luther
Site accessed 12/11/2014

The Ninety-Five Theses
http://en.wikipedia.org/wiki/The_Ninety-Five_Theses
Site accessed 12/11/2014

Protestant Reformation
http://en.wikipedia.org/wiki/Protestant_Reformation
Site accessed 11/7/2014

Church architecture
http://en.wikipedia.org/wiki/Church_architecture#From_house_
church_to_church
Site accessed 12/15/2014

Protestantism
http://en.wikipedia.org/wiki/Protestantism
Site accessed 12/13/2014

Sacrament
http://en.wikipedia.org/wiki/Sacrament
Site accessed 12/13/2014

Ignatius of Antioch
http://en.wikipedia.org/wiki/Ignatius_of_Antioch
Site accessed 12/13/2014

Augsburg Confession
http://en.wikipedia.org/wiki/Augsburg_Confession
Site accessed 12/13/2014

Holy orders (Catholic Church)
http://en.wikipedia.org/wiki/Holy_orders_(Catholic_Church)
Site accessed 12/13/2014

Sacrifice of the Mass
http://www.newadvent.org/cathen/10006a.htm
Site accessed 12/13/2014

Eucharist
http://en.wikipedia.org/wiki/Eucharist
Site accessed 12/15/2014

Eucharist in the Catholic Church
http://en.wikipedia.org/wiki/Eucharist_in_the_Catholic_Church
Site accessed 12/15/2014

Divine Service (Lutheran)
http://en.wikipedia.org/wiki/Divine_Service_(Lutheran)
Site accessed 12/13/2014

Chapter 4 – Confirming Observations

Have you ever had the experience where you were walking somewhere and you approached two people that were having a conversation with each other, and as you got closer, they stopped their conversation and waited until you passed and got farther away from them before they continued their conversation?

Or have you ever been talking with someone when a person you did not know walked by you, and you found that you paused your conversation until the person passed and got farther away from where they could hear you?

My guess is that you have had both of these experiences numerous times, just like I have – as well as others that I know who have also had these experiences.

In both of these examples, 2s-and-3s was hindered by an additional person just getting into the proximity of the 2s-and-3s. So, these are but two examples of why 2s-and-3s tends to be more conducive to heart-to-heart fellowship than are things with larger numbers, including 1-to-many settings.

Will it work with four?

In the next chapter and in the appendix of this book, we will explore how you can facilitate your own Twos and Threes Party as but one way that you can help others to experience the benefits of 2s-and-3s. I mention this now so that the following makes more sense…

A friend of ours came to one of the Twos and Threes Parties we held at our house. Usually this person stays quiet in larger groups, but in the 2s-and-3s times, she shared her heart beautifully and started to shine with joy and a beautiful smile. At one point in the party, we went to split into 2s-and-3s, and her husband, being a very loving and social person, wanted to include more than three people in the group the two of them were in. She then proceeded to say that if there were more than three people, then she would not share. The reason she said this was because she knew that with more people there would be less time for each person to share, and as such she would tend to be quiet so as to allow the others enough time for them to share – even if it would mean that she would not get the opportunity to share.

I have another friend who shared with me how he was frustrated by the fact that when he would go to dinner with his wife and another couple, the two women would chat while both he and the other man would tend to stay quiet. So, even though he wanted to have meaningful conversation with the other man, he was not able to do so. I then shared with him about what Jesus said about 2s-and-3s, and I suggested that he try going out to breakfast or lunch with only him and the other man. He decided it was worth a try. Now many years later he has found that it works so well that he is meeting separately with five different men and is really enjoying the 1-to-1 heart sharing. So, this is another example of where the person found that even with the small size of four people, it would hinder their being able to participate.

Shifting from sharing to teaching at

I have also observed that as a group gets larger that people often shift from the personal sharing of their hearts to instead seeing it as a stage where they have a captive audience. In this they might try to use the group to build their own value by doing such things as trying to show how smart they are or show how funny they are. And they may start to teach at the group, tell the group what the group needs to do, or try to guilt the group to help with their agenda. In other words, it can become a big temptation for the 1 to lord it over the many.

> Jesus called them together and said, "You know that those who are regarded as rulers of the Gentiles **lord it over them**, and their high officials **exercise authority over them**. Not so with you. Instead, whoever wants to become great among you must be your servant, and whoever wants to be first must

be slave of all. For even the Son of Man did not come to be served, but to serve, and to give his life as a ransom for many." (Mark 10:42-45, emphasis mine)

So as a group gets bigger, the temptation of the 1 to lord it over the many tends to increase as well.

I recently saw an example of this when my wife, Bonna, and I were sharing a buffet style meal with a number of people. Everyone first got their meal at the buffet table and then took it to other tables where they would eat it. A person joined the table where Bonna and I were already at, and the person listened and shared nicely. But once the group grew a little larger, the person shifted into telling a joke to his captive audience. I thought it was fascinating to watch. In this instance, the person shifted into a 1-to-many mentality at the point where the group grew from about six to seven people. I have seen this shift to a 1-to-many mentality happen numerous times in other settings as well, but the threshold number where the shift occurs seems to vary on any of a number of factors, such as how well the 1 knows the many or how much the 1 wants an audience.

Looking at the numbers

If we look at the number of people involved, then it can help us to see all of this in an even greater way.

How comfortable would you be sharing very personally with 1 other person? How about 2 others? How about 3 others? How about 4 others? How about 10 others? How about 20 others? How about 100 others? How about 1,000 others?

Since each of us is uniquely created by the Lord, with some of us being more social than others, my guess is that your threshold of how many people you would be comfortable sharing your heart with may be different than my threshold. And it also probably depends on how well you know the people you are sharing with. So, even though your threshold level may be different than mine, overall you would probably find that you are more comfortable sharing your heart with less people than with more people. And the larger the group becomes, the less comfortable you would tend to feel sharing your heart.

Even if people could share their hearts in a 1-to-many setting as well as they could in a 2s-and-3s setting, there is still the practical issue of numbers. For example, if you had 30 minutes for people to share about some topic, and the 30 minutes was divided up evenly for each person to have the same amount of time to share. Then what would that look like for 2, 3, 10, 100, and 1,000 people? Here is the math:

$$30 / 2 = 15 \text{ minutes each}$$

$$30 / 3 = 10 \text{ minutes each}$$

$$30 / 10 = 3 \text{ minutes each}$$

$$30 / 100 = .3 \text{ minutes} = 18 \text{ seconds each}$$

$$30 / 1,000 = .03 \text{ minutes} = 1.8 \text{ seconds each}$$

So, from a practical standpoint, if you had 1 microphone and 1,000 people, and each person shared for 1.8 seconds, it would be difficult to have a deep conversation to say the least.

Conclusion

Overall, I think the practical observations in this chapter reflect how the Lord has designed us for 2s-and-3s fellowship. As you read my observations, I hope you could think of examples in your life where you have also observed how people have interacted differently in 2s-and-3s from how they interacted with larger numbers of people.

In the next chapter we will look at some practical ways for each of us to get lots of good 2s-and-3s fellowship.

Chapter 5 – Practical Applications

If after reading the prior chapters, the initial claim from Chapter 1 now makes all the more sense to you, the claim being:

> **It is of great value for each of us to have the freedom to count twos and threes fellowship as more significant than things that are one to many.**

And from this you have decided that you would like to get more 2s-and-3s fellowship. Then are there practical ways for you to do this? Yes indeed! I hope this chapter gives you some good ideas and that over time Jesus gives you lots of additional ideas that are unique to His best for you.

The first thing I would suggest is a prayer. In other words, that you would ask Jesus to provide you with good 2s-and-3s fellowship since He knows the best times and places for when and where to provide this for you. And He also knows the best pick of people to join you in those 2s-and-3s.

> Dear Jesus,
>
> I ask that You would provide me with lots of good 2s-and-3s fellowship.
>
> Thanks and in Jesus' name,
>
> Your Name

In light of this prayer, here are some ideas that He may lead you to…

In the prior chapter we looked at two ideas. The one was to invite another person to join you for a meal – such as breakfast or lunch. The other was a Twos and Threes Party that you could facilitate to not only provide yourself with 2s-and-3s fellowship, but to also provide this for others as well.

One great thing about 2s-and-3s is that they can happen in so many settings. For example, if we had 1,000 people to gather into one place, then there are many settings where the 1,000 people would **not** fit. But with only two or three people, there are an incredible number of settings that would work. The following are but a few of these:

~ Sitting on chairs.

~ Sitting at a picnic bench.

~ Sitting on rocks overlooking a creek.

~ Standing next to each other.

~ Taking a walk together.

~ Going on a car ride together.

In addition to these settings where you would meet face-to-face with the other one or two people, there are also electronic settings as well, such as by phone or Skype™.

Even in larger settings one can think "2s-and-3s". For example, if you attend a wedding or a high school graduation, before and after the "official time" there are often opportunities for 2s-and-3s. Or if you are at a large table for an event such as a family reunion, there are often lots of 2s-and-3s conversations going on within the larger group. So, if instead of seeing a larger group as one big crowd, you see it as many individuals with the potential for many 2s-and-3s, then there are often 2s-and-3s that you will be able to find within the larger crowd.

Summary

In this short chapter we looked at the great advantage of 2s-and-3s in that they can happen in so many settings, and how Jesus can help guide each of us to good 2s-and-3s fellowship in His unique best for our lives. I hope in reading this chapter you have been able to think of additional possibilities for 2s-and-3s that I did not list, and in all of this that you wind up with lots of excellent 2s-and-3s fellowship!

Chapter 6 – How you can participate better

As you participate in 2s-and-3s fellowship, you may wonder if there are any things that can help you to participate even better. If so, I hope some of the ideas in this chapter will help you to participate better and in turn that the value of 2s-and-3s increases all the more for you as well as for those you are in 2s-and-3s fellowship with. My desire is that Jesus highlights things to you from this chapter that pertain to His best for you, and that over time He personally teaches you additional things that will help you as well. With all of this said, here are some ideas…

Understanding your role

With the 1-to-many model being so prevalent, it can affect how one approaches 2s-and-3s. A person can think that they need to spend all of the 2s-and-3s time teaching the other one or two people. Or a person may be so used to listening to a 1 in a 1-to-many setting that they think they should be a quiet spectator. Both of these positions can work against good 2s-and-3s fellowship.

So, if you find that you are feeling responsible to be the 1 to teach the other one or two people, you may have good intentions in sharing with them, but if they do not get a chance to also share their hearts, it will work against having good 2s-and-3s fellowship. If we look again at the 4-step process, we can see that if you are the only one sharing, then the other one or two people will not be able to participate in all four steps.

> **Step 1:** Jesus works continually in you through His Holy Spirit to both filter and enhance the data coming into you via your senses by giving you a sense of what is best for you to reject, and to give you insights into those things that are best for you to receive.

> But when he, the (Holy) Spirit of truth, comes, he will

guide you into all the truth. (John 16:13a)

For example, when you hear someone speaking you may sense that something is not quite right in what they are saying and therefore it is best to not receive it – hence filtering the data coming into you. Or when someone shares something with you, something might stand out to you as the Holy Spirit gives you insights into it – hence the enhancing of the data coming into you.

Step 2: As you meet with two others, you are now in a 2s-and-3s. The Holy Spirit will work in your mind and heart, and will help you to share your heart with the other two people.

Step 3: As the other two people listen to you share, the Holy Spirit will work in both of them to filter and enhance what you have shared with them so as to uniquely tailor it to each of their lives.

Step 4: The ball of fellowship rolls along as the Holy Spirit helps each person to share their heart with the other two, and the Holy Spirit also filters and enhances the data going into each person.

The other one or two people may benefit from what you share, but they will be missing out on step 4 where they would become full participants instead of being reduced to spectators only. If you have mostly been in 1-to-many settings (especially if you have been the 1 teaching the many), then this shift to a 4-step mutual sharing process may take some time for you to get used to.

This can also happen if you are older by age or have been a Christian longer than the other one or two people. Then if you are used to a discipleship model where most of the time is spent with you teaching the other person, instead of a mutual fellowship discipleship model where the Lord is building everyone up through the fellowship, then you may feel tempted to have to teach the other one or two people. The reason the 4-step process works so well is because the Holy Spirit is working in every step. As such, the youngest person or the person that has been a Christian for the least amount of time can share things that are very significant and help the ball of fellowship to roll along well. For it to work well, it is important for them to participate and for you to participate as well.

On the other hand, if you tend to be shy and often have thoughts like, "They will not want to hear what I have to say." And from this you stay quiet the whole time. Then you will be reduced to a spectator rather than a full participant in the 4-step process. I know some people who have been shy like this, and yet eventually came to love good 2s-and-3s fellowship – with themselves as full participants!

One thing that gave these shy people a greater freedom to share their hearts was realizing that the picture in their mind of how they thought the other one or two people would respond was indeed very different from how it turned out to be. The key in this is realizing that the Holy Spirit is much smarter than we can imagine, knows what is the very best for us to share, and knows how He will use that in the lives of the other one or two people – since He also knows the future. So, as you look to the Holy Spirit to help you in your sharing, you may find it surprising how even the little you share can be of great benefit to the other one or two people. And the more you get used to sharing in 2s-and-3s, the more it can confirm to you that it indeed usually turns out much better than what you had originally envisioned in your mind.

You also may be shy about sharing because you feel like you are less knowledgeable than the other one or two people or that you only have a little to share – almost like having something half-baked in the oven that you do not want to take out until it is fully baked. But if you think about a cat playing with a ball of yarn, it can be very helpful. There may only be a little strand of yarn sticking out from the entire ball of yarn. But if the cat gets ahold of it, then the whole ball may begin to unravel. In a similar way, if you share the little that you have on your heart to share, often as the Holy Spirit makes things alive to the other one or two people, then as they also share, the ball begins to unravel more. This allows the Holy Spirit to work through what each person already knows to cause the combined knowledge to be much greater. And with the ball of fellowship rolling, the Holy Spirit can bring all the other benefits of good 2s-and-3s, such as bringing mutual encouragement to each person. I have often seen where someone shared their "little" and from it the ball of fellowship took off in a great way!

So, if in 2s-and-3s you are in the role of one whom both gives and receives, then it can greatly benefit the 2s-and-3s fellowship that you partake of.

Listening and Sharing

In order to participate well in 2s-and-3s fellowship, both listening and sharing are needed. As such, if one does not listen well to the other one or two people, then what they share will most likely be less relevant to the conversation. If on the other hand, one listens but does not share, then they will be reduced to a spectator only.

Fortunately, the Holy Spirit can help each of us to do well in both listening and sharing. In light of this, I would suggest a prayer.

Dear Jesus,

Please help me to both listen well and share my heart well in any 2s-and-3s fellowship that I partake of.

Thanks and in Jesus' name,

Your Name

Listening

Listening well is a skill that Jesus can grow each of us in, which in turn has many benefits – including those found in 2s-and-3s.

Step 3 of the 4-step process is written from the viewpoint of the other one or two people listening to what you are sharing with them.

> **Step 3:** As the other two people listen to you share, the Holy Spirit will work in both of them to filter and enhance what you have shared with them so as to uniquely tailor it to each of their lives.

But the same applies to you when you are the one listening. As the other person shares, the Holy Spirit will cause things to stand out to you and will help you to know how those things apply to your life. Just knowing this can help you to be encouraged to be all the more sensitive to the Holy Spirit in this listening process. It also benefits the other person who is sharing, since they will feel better understood by you. Also, as you listen this way, it can help you to get a better sense of what would be good for you to share when it is your turn to share.

Sharing

Being sensitive to the Holy Spirit is not only a key for listening but also for sharing as we can see in step 2 of the 4-step process.

> **Step 2:** As you meet with two others, you are now in a 2s-and-3s. The Holy Spirit will work in your mind and heart, and will help you to share your heart with the other two people.

One way the Holy Spirit does this is through inspiration. We can see this in the following verse that refers to prophets, but the same concept more widely applies to non-prophets as well.

> The angel said to me, "These words are trustworthy and true.

The Lord, the **God who inspires the prophets**, sent his angel to show his servants the things that must soon take place." (Revelation 22:6, emphasis mine)

So, often you will find yourself inspired to share something with the other one or two people, and as you do this, the Holy Spirit will often enhance your sharing.

But when they arrest you, **do not worry about what to say or how to say it**. At that time **you will be given what to say, for it will not be you speaking, but the Spirit of your Father speaking through you**. (Matthew 10:19-20, emphasis mine)

As you are sensitive to the Holy Spirit, He will sometimes give you a "check" that something is better to not share. Other times, the Holy Spirit will give you a sense that something is good to share.

There have been times when I ignored the "check" from the Holy Spirit, and as I shared what I thought would be helpful, it totally backfired – showing me that the Holy Spirit truly knows what is the very best for me to share and also how sharing that will play out in the future. Other times, I sensed there would be something good to share, and as I shared it, the other person was very touched in a good way. In light of this, I have at times prayed asking Jesus to help me to be very sensitive to His Holy Spirit. So, feel free to pray this for yourself as well.

Dear Jesus,

Please help me to be very sensitive to Your Holy Spirit so that I share what is good to share and avoid sharing what is best not to share.

Thanks and in Jesus' name,

Your Name

One thing to note about sharing is that if someone does not seem to like what you shared with them, it does not necessarily mean that it would have been better for you to have refrained from sharing it. Instead, it could be that in the long run Jesus uses it to help that person to grow in good ways – even though at first it was a little challenging for them to hear it. So, if I find that something seems to be on my heart to share, and yet it also seems that it could cause the other one or two people to be a little challenged, then I usually first silently check with the Lord to get a confirmation from Him before sharing it. And if I get a "check" from the Holy Spirit about it, then I look to not share it.

Increased Love

The more agape love in a 2s-and-3s, the better off it will tend to be. As such, if everyone feels more loved, then it can be a big boost to mutual encouragement. But if love is lacking, then it will work against good 2s-and-3s fellowship.

> You, my brothers and sisters, were called to be free. **But do not use your freedom to indulge the flesh; rather, serve one another humbly in love. For the entire law is fulfilled in keeping this one command: "Love your neighbor as yourself." If you bite and devour each other, watch out or you will be destroyed by each other.** (Galatians 5:13-15, emphasis mine)

So, there is lots of common sense in the question, "Is it loving for me to share a certain thing?" For example, if something is shared out of hatred, and contains slander and gossip, would it truly benefit 2s-and-3s fellowship? Obviously, not. Instead, if things are only shared if they pass the "agape love test", then it can more easily work toward mutual encouragement and Christian maturity.

> Instead, **speaking the truth in love, we will grow to become in every respect the mature** body of him who is the head,

> that is, Christ. (Ephesians 4:15, emphasis mine)

Overall, this points to the greatest two commandments being integral to good 2s-and-3s fellowship.

> One of the teachers of the law came and heard them debating. Noticing that Jesus had given them a good answer, he asked him, "Of all the commandments, which is the most important?" "The most important one," answered Jesus, "is this: 'Hear, O Israel: The Lord our God, the Lord is one. **Love the Lord your God with all your heart and with all your soul and with all your mind and with all your strength.**' The second is this: '**Love your neighbor as yourself**.' There is no commandment greater than these." (Mark 12:28-31, emphasis mine)

But if there is a lack of love, then it will come out in what is said.

> A good man brings good things out of the good stored up in his heart, and an evil man brings evil things out of the evil stored up in his heart. For the mouth speaks what the heart is full of. (Luke 6:45)

We can see an example of a lack of agape love in the following verses where instead of loving each other, Jesus' disciples were competitively arguing with each other over which of them was the greatest.

> A dispute also arose among them as to which of them was considered to be greatest. Jesus said to them, "The kings of the Gentiles lord it over them; and those who exercise authority over them call themselves Benefactors. But you are not to be like that. Instead, the greatest among you should be like the youngest, and the one who rules like the one who serves? For who is greater, the one who is at the table or the one who serves? Is it not the one who is at the table? But I am among you as one who serves. (Luke 22:24-27)

Without agape love, what one shares can have the flavor of lording it over the one or two other people. This in turn works directly against good 2s-and-3s fellowship. In other words, if I use 2s-and-3s fellowship to try to build my own value by competitively lording things over the other one or two people, then they will most likely be tempted to feel devalued and discouraged through the process, instead of being built up through mutual encouragement.

So if I lack agape love, then my sharing can be noisy like a clanging cymbal to the ears of the other one or two people.

> If I speak in the tongues of men or of angels, **but do not have love, I am only a resounding gong or a clanging cymbal**. If I have the gift of prophecy and can fathom all mysteries and all knowledge, and if I have a faith that can move mountains, **but do not have love, I am nothing. If I** give all I possess to the poor and give over my body to hardship that I may boast, **but do not have love, I gain nothing**. (1 Corinthians 13:1-3, emphasis mine)

But with more agape love, it can help me to keep from unhealthy complaining, where built into my complaints is the rejection of Jesus and others. Instead it can be the healthy sharing of my heart where I can even share what I am troubled by, but in the context of maintaining agape love for Jesus and others – without rejecting Jesus or anyone. This reminds me of Jesus praying in the Garden of Gethsemane where He was in great prayer travail as He poured out His heart to the Father, but in this He never stopped having agape love for the Father.

All of this gets us to this especially challenging part of this chapter, which is the question of, "How can we have more agape love in our 2s-and-3s fellowship?" The key to this is found in the following verses spoken by Jesus:

> I am the true vine, and my Father is the gardener. He cuts off

every branch in me that bears no fruit, while every branch that does bear fruit he prunes so that it will be even more fruitful. You are already clean because of the word I have spoken to you. **Remain in me, as I also remain in you. No branch can bear fruit by itself; it must remain in the vine. Neither can you bear fruit unless you remain in me. I am the vine; you are the branches. If you remain in me and I in you, you will bear much fruit; apart from me you can do nothing.** If you do not remain in me, you are like a branch that is thrown away and withers; such branches are picked up, thrown into the fire and burned. If you remain in me and my words remain in you, ask whatever you wish, and it will be done for you. This is to my Father's glory, that you bear much fruit, showing yourselves to be my disciples. As the Father has loved me, so have I loved you. Now remain in my love. If you keep my commands, you will remain in my love, just as I have kept my Father's commands and remain in his love. I have told you this so that my joy may be in you and that your joy may be complete. My command is this: Love each other as I have loved you. (John 15:1-12, emphasis mine)

From these verses we can see that abiding in Jesus is needed to bear fruit. And agape love is the first fruit of the Spirit listed in Galatians 5.

> **But the fruit of the Spirit is love**, joy, peace, forbearance, kindness, goodness, faithfulness, gentleness and self-control. Against such things there is no law. (Galatians 5:22-23, emphasis mine)

The connection point between us as the branches and Jesus as the Vine is our hearts. If our hearts stay wide open and with Jesus, then agape love and the rest of the fruit of His Holy Spirit can more easily flow through us. The nasty thing about temptation is that to reach for it means that we have to pull our hearts away from Jesus, which in turn will prevent His agape love from flowing through us. The demons hate God (which is a whole other story as to why) and as such they especially hate those who have God's Holy Spirit within them and will use temptation to try to keep us from loving God, others, and ourselves. So, the demons will wrap even seemingly good things in a bad context so that if we take a bite of their temptation, we will wind up breaking fellowship with Jesus. This will in turn keep us from being able to have agape love for God, others, and ourselves. So, the challenge in this is to keep our hearts both wide open to the Lord and also with the Lord. It is only the Lord who can enable us to do this. Therefore, I would suggest a prayer.

> Dear Jesus,
>
> Please increase the amount of Your Holy Spirit within me and gift me with a great measure of Your agape love. In this, please help me to keep my heart fully open to You and with You so that Your love can flow through my heart. And if I stumble into temptation, please help me to turn quickly back to You, ask You to forgive me according to Your work for me on the Cross, and continue to abide well in You and to be a good friend to You as well.
>
> Thanks and in Jesus' name,
>
> Your Name

So, may Jesus grow both you and me into greater measures of His agape love, and in turn may it greatly benefit all of the 2s-and-3s we partake of. And as we get good 2s-and-3s fellowship, we can see from the Chapter 2 benefits, that it can in turn help us to avoid the sin that can torpedo good 2s-and-3s fellowship. In other words, this is a positive cycle where both agape love and 2s-and-3s fellowship increase. So as the agape love increases, it helps the 2s-and-3s fellowship to become even better. And as the 2s-and-3s fellowship becomes even better, it in turn helps our hearts to be even more responsive to the Lord so that our hearts can have even more of Jesus' agape love flowing through them.

Summary

In this chapter we looked at some tips on how we can participate better in 2s-and-3s fellowship. I hope you found some things that were helpful to you, and that you all the more can participate well in good 2s-and-3s fellowship.

Chapter 7 – Summary

The original claim in the introduction stated:

> **It is of great value for each of us to have the freedom to count twos and threes fellowship as more significant than things that are one to many.**

I then went on to say:

> In the rest of this book I will share with you the reasons for this claim. As you read, I hope the Holy Spirit encourages you and uses this book material to establish an anchor of freedom for you to enjoy and be encouraged by 2s-and-3s fellowship all the more.

So, I hope the Holy Spirit has indeed encouraged you through this book and has established an anchor of freedom for you to enjoy and be encouraged by 2s-and-3s all the more!

A Possible Exception?

If you enjoy 2s-and-3s fellowship all the more, someone might say to you that 1-to-many settings are still better than 2s-and-3s – especially if people become Christians in a 1-to-many setting.

I would agree that someone becoming a Christian in **any** setting is amazing because Jesus enabled them to cross over from death to life!

> Very truly I (Jesus) tell you, whoever hears my word and believes him who sent me has eternal life and will not be judged but has crossed over from death to life. (John 5:24)

And if this occurs in a 1-to-many setting, then it is definitely a great value of that 1-to-many setting!

But if instead of looking at this possible exception from a large group macro level, we look at it from a personal micro level, then it becomes apparent that if someone only attends 1-to-many settings but is not primarily partaking of 2s-and-3s, then they are missing out on steps 2 through 4 of the four-step process. And since they are not participating in and growing in 2s-and-3s, they will be less full of the Lord, and in turn less useful in 1-to-many settings. In other words, if they are not getting good 2s-and-3s fellowship, then they will not love the many as well. The reason for this is because good 2s-and-3s fellowship will help them to abide better in the Vine of Jesus which in turn is needed for them to have the fruit of the Holy Spirit flowing through them. And love is the first fruit of the Holy Spirit.

And if the person happens to be the 1 sharing the Gospel, then even if people become Christians, they still will not feel as loved as they could. Hence the person will not be as good of an ambassador for Christ as they could be if they were getting more 2s-and-3s fellowship.

So once again, it is truly good for all of us to count 2s-and-3s as more important than 1-to-many.

With this exception now addressed, I close by saying that my heart's desire is that all of us would truly have wonderful 2s-and-3s fellowship in many places and in many ways! And through the 2s-and-3s, we would all the more grow in and experience wonderful friendships with Jesus and each other!

Thank you for letting me share my heart with you through this book material. I hope Jesus continues to use this book in your life in good ways.

Scott

Appendix – How to have a Twos and Threes Party

We had a Twos and Threes Party at our house one night and at one point I listened to all of the wonderful heart sharing that was occurring in the many 2s-and-3s settings in the basement and first floor. I was so touched in realizing the Holy Spirit was working in all of those 2s-and-3s to encourage, build up, and grow friendships among the people. In contrast, I pictured in my mind all of those same people instead being in a 1-to-many setting as silent spectators and not experiencing the many benefits of 2s-and-3s fellowship. This caused me to be all the more thankful for all of the great 2s-and-3s fellowship going on!

When we talk about having another Twos and Threes Party, my wife and adult children get excited in anticipating both themselves and others being so very blessed like they and others have been in prior Twos and Threes Parties. And others have felt the same way, such as a friend of ours who attended her first Twos and Threes Party, and near the end of the party she shared how she had been looking for this very thing for forty years and had now found it!

It is one thing for a person to try to conceptually understand the value of 2s-and-3s fellowship. But in some ways, it is easier for the person to understand the value if they experience it in person. So, hosting a Twos and Threes Party can provide this first-hand experience for all of those who participate in it. As such, you might think that you would like to try hosting a Twos and Threes Party to provide this for both yourself and others, but you may be uncertain as to if you could actually do so, since maybe you are a new Christian and feel like you do not know enough of the Bible, or perhaps you are a little bit shy. Fortunately, hosting a Twos and Threes Party is easier than it might sound since it relies more on facilitation than on teaching. So after you read the rest of this appendix, hopefully it will sound even more doable to you. But, Jesus is the One who ultimately knows how you would do and what is best. So, I would first suggest a prayer.

Dear Jesus,

As I read the rest of this appendix, please help me to know if You would like me to host one or more Twos and Threes Parties. I ask this according to Your James 1:5 promise for wisdom, including wisdom for guidance.

> If any of you lacks wisdom, you should ask God, who gives generously to all without finding fault, and it will be given to you. (James 1:5)

Thanks and in Jesus' name,

Your Name

Facilitator versus Teacher

One of the keys to holding a Twos and Threes Party is to understand that a Facilitator is needed instead of a Teacher. In other words, in many 1-to-many settings, the 1 teaches the many. As such, the 1 is often quite knowledgeable about what they are teaching. But the goal of a Twos and Threes Party is to have lots of 2s-and-3s fellowship. As such, being an "expert" is not required like it is in some teaching-oriented settings. Instead, in a Twos and Threes Party the Facilitator does not have to be an expert but just helps to get the fellowship ball rolling and trusts the Holy Spirit to work through the 2s-and-3s times.

In light of this, the Facilitator's overall role is to introduce topics to everyone gathered in one large group, help everyone to split into 2s-and-3s, participate in a 2s-and-3s just like anyone else, bring the 2s-and-3s back to the large group, and then repeat the process a few more times. The detailed steps for the Facilitator are outlined at the end of this appendix. But for now we will explore things that would help the Facilitator to do well.

Facilitator Tips

Since the Facilitator is facilitating instead of teaching, they will only need to introduce each topic by sharing about it for at most ten minutes instead of their having to do a longer teaching on it. But if the Facilitator is uncomfortable introducing topics, they can ask others to do this for them. The instructions for how to delegate a topic are outlined later in this appendix.

Another thing the Facilitator does is to protect the group from someone who may try to take over the large group times. Fortunately, the Twos and Threes Party is designed to minimize the number of large group times in favor of having many 2s-and-3s times. As such, it is more difficult for someone to try to take over the large group times. But if someone does try to do so, the Facilitator can politely say something like, "That seems like an interesting topic. Would you mind waiting until Snack Time later so that everyone can first participate in 2s-and-3s fellowship? And then at Snack Time others who are interested can join you for discussion." Please note that in rare circumstances, the Facilitator may find that the Lord guides them to allow the person to continue their sharing – like if the person is very distraught by their getting a text message telling them that one of their close relatives has died. Besides this type of exception, it is best for the Facilitator to keep the 2s-and-3s fellowship ball rolling so that **everyone** can fully benefit from having lots of 2s-and-3s time. Overall, Jesus can help the Facilitator to know what to do, such as deferring a topic to Snack Time, so that people do not see the Facilitator as a prison warden with a club, and at the same time 2s-and-3s fellowship can be protected.

Many things from *Chapter 6 – How you can participate better* apply to good facilitation. For example, the more of God's love the Facilitator has flowing through them to the group, the more those in the group will feel loved and valued. This will also help them to feel safer about the whole setting, and in turn they will most likely feel safer about sharing their hearts with others in 2s-and-3s.

If instead of the Facilitator seeing themselves as a Facilitator, they see themselves as the Leader or Teacher of the group, then a number of temptations may follow. In writing this, I am not assuming that if you decide to facilitate, that you would fall into these temptations. But just knowing that you could be tempted in such ways, can make it easier to avoid such temptations. We can see this in the verses we looked at in Chapter 6 about the temptation to lord things over others.

> A dispute also arose among them as to which of them was considered to be greatest. Jesus said to them, "**The kings of the Gentiles lord it over them**; and those who exercise authority over them call themselves Benefactors. **But you are not to be like that. Instead, the greatest among you should be like the youngest, and the one who rules like the one who serves.** For who is greater, the one who is at the table or the one who serves? Is it not the one who is at the table? But I am among you as one who serves. (Luke 22:24-27, emphasis mine)

Since the Facilitator uses speech in their facilitating, it provides the Facilitator with a speaking platform. If the Facilitator uses that platform to try to build their own value by lording it over the others, it will tend to cause the other people to feel devalued. This in turn can cause the people to feel tempted to reject what the Facilitator shares.

An example of lording it over others would be the Facilitator saying something like, "this is what you must do, go think about it!" When the other people feel demanded upon in such a way, they can feel devalued, and in turn they can reject what is being said in order to try to preserve their value. So even if what the Facilitator shares is something good, but it has a lord-it-over-others feel to it, it still might get rejected and be argued against by the hearers. But if the Facilitator has a humbler, personal attitude and says something like, "I am learning about this, the Lord is growing me in this area, and I am finding this topic to be very valuable to me." Then the Facilitator would be modeling a better pattern for sharing that people might more easily take into their 2s-and-3s times.

So, how would you feel if a Facilitator said the following to you?

> "I am an expert on this topic and you must listen to me! You better pay attention if you are going to learn to master this topic as I have!"

I imagine you might not appreciate being talked to in such a way.

Instead, how would you feel if a Facilitator said the following to you?

> "I have been finding the following thoughts to be quite interesting. The more I learn about it, the more I am excited to learn and grow all the more in it. You may have more insights about this than I do, and I hope in your 2s-and-3s you will have great discussion about it."

My guess is that you would prefer to be talked to this way rather than in the earlier "I am an expert" way.

If the Facilitator takes this nicer, non-lording-it-over tone in what they share as the "Facilitator", instead of as the "Expert Teacher", then this humbler tone can help them to not undermine their role as the Facilitator.

> When he (Jesus) noticed how the guests picked the places of honor at the table, he told them this parable: "When someone invites you to a wedding feast, do not take the place of honor, for a person more distinguished than you may have been invited. If so, the host who invited both of you will come and say to you, 'Give this person your seat.' Then, humiliated, you will have to take the least important place. But when you are invited, **take the lowest place**, so that when your host comes, he will say to you, 'Friend, move up to a better place.' Then you will be honored in the presence of all the other guests. For

all those who exalt themselves will be humbled, and those who humble themselves will be exalted." (Luke 14:7-11, emphasis mine)

From this "lower place", the people will tend to appreciate the helpful facilitation, and it can in turn help everyone to more easily attain the many benefits of the 2s-and-3s fellowship – especially since they are not being troubled by someone trying to lord things over them.

Overall, the Twos and Threes Party is a catalyst to help people get going with 2s-and-3s so that they can then continue to get good 2s-and-3s fellowship beyond the life of the Twos and Threes Party. So, if the Facilitator can trust that the Holy Spirit will work in many ways during and after the entire Twos and Threes Party, then it can make it easier for them to not feel like they have to make the evening work. Instead, they can relax more and let the all-powerful, awesome Holy Spirit work in wonderful ways!

Some stuff built in

There are a number of things built into the Twos and Threes Party to make it easier on the Facilitator and to help the Twos and Threes Party to go well. So, if you do end up facilitating, you may want to know about these things so that it makes your facilitation easier and can help you to preserve the valuable things that can come out of a Twos and Threes Party.

The Twos and Threes Party is designed to scale well in size. It is designed to handle 6, 10, 20, or even 100 people. The way this is done is for the Facilitator to be the main speaker in the large group times instead of opening the large group times up for everyone to share. For example, if there were 100 people and in the large group the Facilitator let all 100 people share what they got out of their 2s-and-3s times, it could take a long time. It might also increase the temptation for a person to use the other 99 people as their audience for their 30 minute sermon. To avoid this, the Facilitator splits the group again into 2s-and-3s where each person can share what they got out of their prior 2s-and-3s time. This in turn allows everyone more time to share their hearts and it helps to avoid people trying to take over.

Someone may feel like the Twos and Threes Party is not official enough because unlike many 1-to-many settings, it does not have large group worship music and prayer. The reason why these are missing is so that more time can be spent in 2s-and-3s fellowship. This in turn allows for all of the benefits of good 2s-and-3s to come forth. And if people are really encouraged through the fellowship, then later at Snack Time some people may be inspired to have a worship time where they give thanks and praise to Jesus in song. And some other people might gather for a time of prayer. So the nice thing about Snack Time later in the evening is that it allows people to do different things such as enjoying the snack, fellowshipping together, and also doing worship and prayer.

One of the great values of a Twos and Threes Party is that it is a onetime event rather than a reoccurring event. This helps it to stay "fresh" and conducive to mutually encouraging 2s-and-3s fellowship. If on the other hand it occurred every day of the week, then it could easily become a heavy demand upon the people that they could feel worn out by. Instead of being refreshingly encouraged, it could lead to people becoming discouraged. It is like having a five course meal. If it was a onetime event, people would most likely enjoy the meal. But if it was a daily event, then how many days would it take before it began to tire out both those hosting it as well as those coming to it?

So, it is a freedom for the Facilitator to see each Twos and Threes Party as a onetime, standalone event and for the Facilitator to look to Jesus for when to have the next Twos and Threes Party. It could be that in a given season the Facilitator has quite a number of Twos and Threes Parties. And yet in another season they may have hardly any or even none. So, if the Facilitator looks to Jesus for James 1:5 wisdom for when to have the next party, it can help it be an event that everyone looks forward to instead of something they dread.

Another thing that helps with this is the suggested invitation email described later in this appendix. Instead of putting a strong demand on people for them to have to attend the Twos and Threes Party, it gives them the total freedom to attend or not. This goes along with the following verse.

> Each of you should give what you have decided in your heart to give, **not reluctantly or under compulsion, for God loves a cheerful giver**. (2 Corinthians 9:7, emphasis mine)

So, if people freely want to attend instead of begrudgingly attending, it will help the whole atmosphere of the Twos and Threes Party.

Overall, the Twos and Threes Party is designed to help the fellowship ball to get rolling for each person. It is like in the game of pool where the queue ball is hit into the racked balls, and all of the balls start rolling in their own direction. In a similar way, the Twos and Threes Party helps to get the 2s-and-3s fellowship balls rolling which will then hopefully continue to roll in the lives of each person. The Twos and Threes Party is also like the shell of a snail. The snail only uses the shell as long as it is alive. In a similar way, the Twos and Threes Party helps people to better experience 2s-and-3s fellowship, but after the party the shell can be thrown away since it has served its purpose. If the shell instead had to be maintained, it would become something that could be tiring for the people to maintain in an ongoing way. The structure is good if it serves its purpose but does not put an ongoing demand upon the people.

Are you ready to be the Facilitator?

So, let us say you feel inspired to facilitate a Twos and Threes Party. You especially like the idea that each Twos and Threes Party is a onetime, standalone event. As such, you pray about it and decide to try it once to see how it goes. Then sometime after the party you can pray again and decide if it would be good to have another Twos and Threes Party. In light of this, if you pray about it and feel like it would be good to try your hand at facilitation, then here are the eight steps needed. And may Jesus richly bless the fellowship!

Step 1: Before taking the actions described in steps 2 through 8, please first read from here to the end of this appendix so that you can first understand all the steps in this 8-step process and also familiarize yourself with the details of the *Twos and Threes Party – Facilitator's Guide* (which is at the end of this appendix).

Step 2: Pray about when to have the Twos and Threes Party. One thing to consider is that a Friday night or Saturday night often works best because people are more willing to stay up late on those nights. But more important than this is for Jesus to help you to know what date would be best.

Step 3: Make an Invitation List and check with the Lord to see if He would like any additions or deletions.

Step 4: Send an email to all of those on your Invitation List that looks something like the following, but with the underlined text changed to the appropriate values (and with the underlines removed).

> Subject: **Twos and Threes Party on Saturday, May 3rd**
>
> Greetings,
>
> We/I felt inspired by Jesus to have a Twos and Threes Party at our/my house/apartment this coming Saturday, May 3rd. We/I prayed about it, and felt a confirmation from the Lord that it indeed would be good to do. So, we/I then prayed about whom to invite and you were included on the list!
>
> A key verse for the evening is, "For where two or three gather in my name, there am I with them. (Matthew 18:20)" So we

will be leveraging this 2s-and-3s model in a desire that through the fellowship of 2s-and-3s gathered in Jesus' name, that everyone would be very encouraged and really enjoy the time together!

The way we will do this is to introduce topics in the large group times and to break into 2s-and-3s to share with each other about the topics. This will allow everyone to share in the 2s-and-3s times instead of having most of their time spent quietly listening to only one person.

This all adds up to the "Twos and Threes Party"!

So if you would like to join <u>us/me</u>, <u>we/I</u> would love for you to be a part of it!

Please note three things:

> **1.** There is no need for you to RSVP, but you are certainly welcome to do so.

> **2.** There is zero demand from <u>us/me</u> for you to attend. <u>We/I</u> truly would like you to have the freedom to do whatever Jesus shows you would be His best for you to do.

> **3.** If you do attend and wonder if you can bring others with you… the answer is yes.

In case you decide to come, here are the directions to <u>our/my</u> place:

> ~ <u>Drive here</u>

> ~ <u>Turn there</u>

~ <u>Go here</u>

~ <u>Park here</u>

Arrival time is after supper anywhere between 6:30 PM to 7:00 PM on <u>Saturday, May 3rd</u>. We will then start the Twos and Threes Party at 7:00 PM. Although dinner is not included, <u>we/I</u> will provide snacks later on. So, there is no need for you to bring a snack – although <u>we/I</u> will not object if you do decide to bring a snack anyway.

With Jesus' love,

<u>Your Name</u>

<u>Your Contact information including</u>
<u>Street Address</u>
<u>Phone Numbers</u>

Step 5: Pray about and determine the Session 3 and Session 5 topics, and check with the Lord to see if it would be good for you to subcontract someone to help with a topic. If yes, then days in advance of the actual party, contact the person to see if they are willing to help. Let them know a little about the Twos and Threes Party and that you would like them to introduce a session by sharing a little on a topic of their choice to get the fellowship ball rolling. It would also be good to let them know that they are only sharing for at most 10 minutes, and after they introduce the topic they can then look back to you for you to break the group into 2s-and-3s. You may also want to consider showing them the appendix of this book so they can get a little better idea about the Twos and Threes Party.

Step 6: Prepare the Snack. Possibly get someone to help you.

Step 7: Set up 2s-and-3s areas. Possibly get someone to help you.

Note: How many 2s-and-3s areas to set up depends on a number of things, such as how many people are expected (approximately), the types of chairs, couches, or benches available, and the place the party is being held – such as in a house, apartment, garage, or outdoors. One thing that is helpful to know is that the large group area can also be used for 2s-and-3s. So, when we have had Twos and Threes Parties at our house, a number of the 2s-and-3s used the large group living room area, while others went to various places that had 3s set up so that they could handle a 2s or a 3s. This included 3s set up in the dining room, kitchen, basement, and the back porch with most of the 3s being either three chairs facing each other in a triangle or a chair facing a couch (to hold 1 on the chair and 2 on the couch).

Step 8: Have a great Twos and Threes Party!

Note: What follows is a step-by-step guide that you can use and modify to suit to facilitate an actual Twos and Threes Party.

Twos and Threes Party – Facilitator's Guide

6:30 PM to 7:00 PM – Arrival.

7:00 PM to an unknown time later – The Twos and Threes Party.

Facilitator to share in the large group
Welcome. First a note about facilities.

~ The bathroom is located at _____

~ _____

A key verse for this evening is, "For where two or three gather in my name, there am I with them. (Matthew 18:20)". So, we are leveraging this 2s-and-3s model in a desire that through the fellowship of the 2s-and-3s gathered in Jesus' name, that everyone would be very encouraged and really enjoy the time together!

If you are wondering why we are focusing upon 2s-and-3s, the reasons are outlined in the book titled *Twos and Threes* written by Scott Brooks (available at www.BrooksFamilyStore.com). The book shows how 2s-and-3s is outlined in the Bible as the main building block for Christian fellowship. And it explains how in the time of Roman Emperor Constantine there was a historic shift away from 2s-and-3s to often be upstaged by 1-to-many models of gathering. The drawback with this is that it tends to be much more difficult in 1-to-many settings to get to the mutually encouraging heart-to-heart fellowship of 2s-and-3s. The reasons for this are somewhat intuitive and are more fully explained in the book. The book also gives many examples of how people can gather in 2s-and-3s. This includes the book's appendix that gives instructions to the reader on how they can host their own Twos and Threes Party – like the one we are having tonight.

With this now explained, I will next share some details to give you an idea of how tonight's Twos and Threes Party is designed to work. As I share this, there is no need for you to take notes or to try to remember it all since as the evening rolls along, I will repeat each step at its appropriate time.

~ Overall, topics will be introduced in this larger group that we are currently in. We will then split into 2s-and-3s where each of us can share with the others about the topic.

~ The way we will split into 2s-and-3s is by asking Jesus to show us who we are to get together with. If you have a hard time discerning this, it is not a problem since most likely someone will pick you. But if you are not picked right away, you can simply wait until the end and join any group of 2. Once a group of 3 is established, they can then go off to where the 2s-and-3s locations are set up at _____. If you are in a group of only 2, please wait until the end so that someone can easily join you to make a group of 3. And if you are shy and do not feel like sharing, you can simply join a group of 2 and observe.

~ After giving the 2s-and-3s some time to fellowship, I will then look to Jesus for when to gather everyone back to the large group. Once we are back in the large group, we will again split into 2s-and-3s where you will most likely be with different people than in your prior 2s-and-3s time. In this second group of 2s-and-3s we will first share with each other about what we got out of our last 2s-and-3s time. If there is any time left over, people can share whatever else is on their hearts that they would like to talk about.

~ I will then look to Jesus for when to gather everyone back to the large group where this process will repeat two more times but with two new topics.

~ After the last 2s-and-3s time, I will gather everyone back to the large group where in the large group anyone can then briefly share what they got out of their 2s-and-3s times or out of our entire time together.

~ This will be followed by a snack time where everyone is free to snack and fellowship for as long as they would like to.

Optional: Facilitator only prayer
Before continuing, I thought it would be nice if I lifted up a short prayer to invite Jesus into our time. Dear Jesus, ... [your prayer here] ... In Jesus' name.

Optional: Facilitator to introduce everyone
I would like to quickly introduce each person by giving their name and where I know them from.
Note to the Facilitator: If you do not know someone, then just ask them their name and where they are from.
Note to the Facilitator: If everyone already knows each other, then you can simply skip this "introduce everyone" part. Or if the group is really large, then you may want to skip this part since it may take too long and the people will get to know each other in the 2s-and-3s anyway. But if the group is not too large and you decide to introduce everyone, you may want to do the introductions yourself since if you allow people to share in the larger group they might **not** keep it brief. Instead they may take the opportunity to introduce themselves for 30 minutes!

Facilitator to share in the large group about Session 1: In this first session we will **not** have a topic introduced like there will be in the subsequent sessions. Instead we will break into groups of 2s-and-3s where each person can introduce themselves. And after everyone introduces themselves, each person can share a prayer request or two, and then everyone can pray for each other. Please note that one goal of praying for each other is to help us to be less loaded up with things so that we can better enjoy the evening together. And please feel free to **not** pray unless you really feel comfortable praying for others.

Facilitator action: Ask the group to split into 2s-and-3s according to the instructions listed earlier of:

> "The way we will split into 2s-and-3s is by asking the Lord to show us who we are to get together with. If you have a hard time discerning this, it is not a problem since most likely someone will pick you. But if you are not picked right away, you can simply wait until the end and join any group of 2. Once a group of 3 is established, they can then go off to where the 2s-and-3s locations are set up at _____. If you are in a group of only 2, please wait until the end so that someone can easily join you to make a group of 3. And if you are shy and do not feel like sharing, you can simply join a group of 2 and observe."

Facilitator action: Look to Jesus for when to gather everyone back to the large group, and once He gives you the go-ahead, then leave the 2s-and-3s group you are in and go around and invite each 2s-and-3s group back to the large group.

Facilitator to share in the large group about Session 2: We will now break into another 2s-and-3s to discuss what each of us got out of our prior 2s-and-3s time. If any time is left over, feel free to share whatever is on your hearts with each other.

Facilitator action: Ask the group to split into 2s-and-3s according to the instructions listed earlier.

Facilitator action: Look to Jesus for when to gather everyone back to the large group, and once He gives you the go-ahead, then leave the 2s-and-3s group you are in and go around and invite each 2s-and-3s group back to the large group.

Facilitator to share in the large group about Session 3: In this session, the topic of _____will be introduced by _____and then we will split into 2s-and-3s where each person can share how what was shared about the topic touched them.

Note to the Facilitator: The goal at this point is to introduce a topic for at most 10 minutes and then to split the group into 2s-and-3s where the fellowship ball can roll nicely. If you asked someone else to introduce the topic, then after they do so, they should then look to you as the Facilitator for you to let the rest of the group know it is time to split into 2s-and-3s.

Facilitator action: Ask the group to split into 2s-and-3s according to the instructions listed earlier.

Facilitator action: Look to Jesus for when to gather everyone back to the large group, and once He gives you the go-ahead, then leave the 2s-and-3s group you are in and go around and invite each 2s-and-3s group back to the large group.

Facilitator to share in the large group about Session 4: We will now break into another 2s-and-3s to discuss what each of us got out of our prior 2s-and-3s time. If any time is left over, feel free to share whatever is on your hearts with each other.

Facilitator action: Ask the group to split into 2s-and-3s according to the instructions listed earlier.

Facilitator action: Look to Jesus for when to gather everyone back to the large group, and once He gives you the go-ahead, then leave the 2s-and-3s group you are in and go around and invite each 2s-and-3s group back to the large group.

Facilitator to share in the large group about Session 5: In this session, the topic of _____will be introduced by _____and then we will split into 2s-and-3s where each person can share how what was shared about the topic touched them.

Note to the Facilitator: The goal at this point is to introduce a topic for at most 10 minutes and then to split the group into 2s-and-3s where the fellowship ball can roll nicely. If you asked someone else to introduce the topic, then after they do so, they should then look to you as the Facilitator for you to let the rest of the group know it is time to split into 2s-and-3s.

Facilitator action: Ask the group to split into 2s-and-3s.

Facilitator action: Look to Jesus for when to gather everyone back to the large group, and once He gives you the go-ahead, then leave the 2s-and-3s group you are in and go around and invite each 2s-and-3s group back to the large group.

Facilitator to share in the large group about Session 6: We will now break **one last time** into another 2s-and-3s to discuss what each of us got out of our prior 2s-and-3s time. If any time is left over, feel free to share whatever is on your hearts with each other.

Facilitator action: Ask the group to split into 2s-and-3s.

Facilitator action: Look to Jesus for when to gather everyone back to the large group, and once He gives you the go-ahead, then leave the 2s-and-3s group you are in and go around and invite each 2s-and-3s group back to the large group.

Facilitator to share in the large group about Session 7: This is our last large group time before going into a snack time. Would anyone like to share a little bit about what you got out of your 2s-and-3s times or what you got out of the entire evening so far?

Facilitator to introduce Snack Time: You are all free to get a snack and hang out as long as you would like to do so.

WOULD YOU LIKE TO SEE
AN AMAZING
MIRACLE?

SCOTT & BONNA BROOKS

Would you like to see an Amazing Miracle?

By Scott and Bonna Brooks

www.SeeMiracle.com

ISBN 978-1-6230946-3-8

Table of Contents for Book 2 –
Would you like to see an Amazing Miracle?

Introduction

Maybe you have never seen a miracle before and have always wanted to. Or maybe you have seen miracles before and think they are fantastic, so you would love to see another miracle. Or maybe you are just curious about miracles. For whatever reason, if you would like to see an amazing miracle, there is a really good chance that you will get to see one now! For there is a very common and yet amazing miracle that has been happening all over the place, and hopefully you can now see it with your own eyes and experience it for yourself! The reason we say "hopefully you can now see it" instead of "you will definitely see it" is because a relatively small percentage of people do not have the physical differences, described in the next section, that are needed for the miracle to occur, and there is also a small percentage of people for whom the miracle does not seem to work for some unknown reason. If you wind up being in this second "unknown reason" category, we certainly would not want you to feel bad about it. But with this disclaimer in place, **feel free to read on** to see if this amazing miracle will work for you!

Please note that what follows is written as if you are in the high percentage of people for whom the miracle will actually work...

Miracle Description

Most people have different length legs where one leg is at least one-quarter inch shorter than the other, and usually it is closer to one-half inch difference or more. Over many years of walking, the shorter leg bears more weight and in turn can cause both leg and back problems, especially for the shorter leg that has taken more of the weight burden, and also for the back on the opposite side of the shorter leg. People go over and over again to expensive chiropractors to try to help with these problems, but this amazing miracle solves the leg difference problem by having the shorter leg grow out to the exact length of the longer leg – in just seconds! And if people have had leg and back pain due to the leg length difference, that pain often goes away as well!

We find this miracle especially amazing when we think about all of the different parts of the leg that instantly grow: skin, bones, muscles, ligaments, cartilage, etc.!

Another result of this miracle is that the person becomes taller due to the leg growth. This can be nice for their being able to reach things they just could not quite reach before, and also for seeing over things that they were not quite tall enough to see over. A bonus result is that the person's feet often grow out to equal lengths, too!

One thing to note is that some people would rather be shorter than taller. Fortunately, this miracle can be done to shorten a longer leg instead of growing a shorter leg. So if you would prefer to be shorter instead of taller, then please adjust the following instructions accordingly.

Legal Disclaimer

The instructions that follow are safe, and yet it is possible that as you do them, someone carrying a cup of very hot coffee could walk into the room you are in, trip over you, and scald you with the coffee. So, we hope you are not offended that we took this precautionary step to safeguard ourselves against some lawsuit-happy person (we assume that is not you). As such, we worked out the following legal disclaimer with a lawyer from a well known law firm:

> Although we hope for good results for you through the steps that follow, we do not in any way guarantee particular results or assume any liability for injuries sustained while completing the steps.

With this said, we will now continue with the instructions...

Preparation for the Miracle

First we need a volunteer who would like to have their legs become the same length. So as long as you are willing to see this miracle on yourself, we are all set – assuming that your legs are different lengths (later we will explain an easy way to see if your legs are the same or different lengths). But if you would rather not be the miracle recipient, or if later when measuring leg lengths, you find that your legs are the same length, then maybe you could find a friend or family member that would like to see the miracle on themselves. If the volunteer is not you, then you can easily adjust the steps for the miracle to work on them instead of you.

Now assuming you are the volunteer, and that you indeed have different length legs, you will have all the benefits described earlier, plus the added benefit of feeling your leg grow out – which is an interesting feeling as things grow and move around. And just in case you are concerned about pain, it might feel a little strange as things grow, but it will not hurt at all!

In addition to the volunteer, you will need two things that will be helpful in determining leg length difference. One is a wall that you can sit against, and the other is something to wear on your feet that have a firm heel – such as a pair of sneakers, shoes, or boots.

To prepare for the miracle, you will first need to determine which leg is longer. Please take the following steps to determine this:

> **1.** Sit on the floor with your back firmly against a wall and your legs outstretched.
>
> Note: If you do not have an available wall nearby that has a clearing wide enough for you to sit against with your legs outstretched, you could instead sit against a closed closet door or even a piece of furniture such as a couch – just as long as it has an even surface for you to sit against that will not move.

Note: If your body is not flexible and you therefore find it difficult to sit with your back firmly against a wall with your legs flat on the ground, you could instead sit in a non-rolling chair with a firm seat and back, outstretch your legs as much as they will permit you to, and place your feet on the floor.

2. Place your legs together.

3. Put the heels of your feet together.

4. Point the toes of each foot away from the other, but keep your heels together so that it is easy to see your heels (making a V shape with your feet).

5. At the point of the V where your heels touch, look at the bottom of your heels to see which of your legs is shorter and which one is longer. In other words, the heel that is furthest away from your eyes (i.e. the heel that sticks out furthest) is part of your longer leg.

Note: If you are having a hard time seeing this clearly, you may want to ask someone to check it for you, since they could take a closer look at your heels than you can in how you are sitting.

Also, you may feel like doing a height comparison to see how much your height changes as a result of the miracle. If you have a standard way to measure your height, you may want to make note of your height before the miracle so that you can then compare it to your height after the miracle. If you do not have a standard way to measure your height, you can use the following alternative technique that will not give you your exact height change, but will at least give you a way to compare the change. To do this alternative technique, just take off your sneakers/shoes/boots and socks, take a pencil or pen, stand near a wall with your feet flat on the ground and with your big toes touching the wall. Reach as high as you can with the arm that is on the same side as your shorter leg. Place the hand of that arm on the wall as high as you can but with your feet still flat on the floor. Lastly, with the pencil or pen in your other hand, mark the wall above the middle finger of the hand you have against the wall. After the leg growing miracle you can do this again to see the difference between the new line and the old line.

Besides measuring your height, you may also want to see if your feet are different lengths, since often with this miracle, the shorter foot will grow out to the length of the longer foot. So if you would like to compare the length of your feet, all you need to do is to take off your sneakers/shoes/boots and socks, stand with your back against a wall, put the heels of your feet against the wall, put your big toes from each foot next to each other, and see which one is longer.

Lastly, once you see the miracle you may possibly begin to question what you saw, since such miracles may be outside of your normal way of looking at things. So, feel free to ask a friend or family member if they would like to see the miracle occur. This way you can compare notes after seeing the miracle to determine if you both observed the same thing.

Now with all of this preparation done, you are ready to see the miracle...

Doing the Miracle

So on your feet, you are wearing something with firm heels (such as a pair of sneakers, shoes, or boots), you are sitting on the floor with your back firmly against the wall, your legs are outstretched, your heels are together, but your toes from each foot are pointed away from each other (making a V shape with your feet), and you have been able to determine which leg is shorter by looking at the heels of your feet.

Now to do the miracle, you will need to use a key name that has the needed authority to cause miracles to happen. In other words, none of us can make this miracle occur on our own, but fortunately, we are permitted to use a key name that has tremendous authority to cause miracles to happen! This is similar to a child not having money for a bus ride, but their parent pays for two tickets and gives one ticket to the child right before the two of them get on the bus. As the child gives the ticket to the bus driver, the bus driver accepts and honors the ticket as sufficient passage and in turn allows the child to take a seat on the bus. Similarly, this key name gives you the rights needed for this miracle to occur. Later on we will let you know why this key name worked for this miracle, but for now, you can get even more value out of this miracle by first trying other names that will not work. So with your right hand on the thigh of your shorter leg, feel free to say any of the following sentences that use names that will not work.

In the name of Elvis Presley, left/right leg grow out.

In the name of Michael Jackson, left/right leg grow out.

In the name of Mickey Mouse, left/right leg grow out.

In the name of Buddha, left/right leg grow out.

In the name of Allah, left/right leg grow out.

In the name of Vishnu, left/right leg grow out.

In the name of the Great Spirit in the sky, left/right leg grow out.

In the name of Mary, left/right leg grow out.

In the name of Mother Teresa, left/right leg grow out.

In the name of Baha'u'llah, left/right leg grow out.

So far, you did not see any change of leg length, correct?

Feel free to try other names as well…

In the name of _____, left/right leg grow out.

Warning: What follows uses a key name that when you hear it, may invoke negative thoughts and/or feelings within you. But, we assure you that the name is absolutely wonderful and is a key to so much more that we will explain later.

If you happened to have already used the key name that we will describe next, then you most likely just saw the miracle. But if you have not yet used this key name, please now try the key name that works by putting your right hand on the thigh of your shorter leg and saying:

In the name of Jesus, left/right leg grow out.

Wow, did you just see an amazing miracle? If so, not only did your shorter leg grow to the exact length of your longer leg, but you are also now taller than before! So if you are doing a standard height comparison, you can now measure your new height to see the difference. And if you are using the alternative height comparison technique described earlier, you can now draw a new line to see the difference between the old line and the new line.

Also, if earlier you had compared the length of your feet and now you would like to check to see if your shorter foot grew, you can compare your foot length by first taking off your sneakers/shoes/boots and socks. Then stand with your back against a wall, put the heels of your feet against the wall, put your big toes from each foot next to each other, and see if they are now the same length. If so, then great! If not, sometimes the miracle happens in two parts: one part for the leg and the second part for the foot. Therefore, if your feet are still different lengths, feel free to put your right hand on your shorter foot and say, "In the name of Jesus, foot grow out." Did you just now see another miracle? If so, super!

And if you had back pain, if you walk around, is it better now? If so, then yea!

Assuming that you just now saw at least one amazing miracle with your leg growing out, the big question becomes: Why did the miracle actually work?

In the next section we will explore what we consider to be both a fascinating and amazing explanation. So, if you would like to know why, **please feel free to read on**. If not, we are glad for you that you at least hopefully enjoyed seeing an amazing miracle!

Miracle Explanation

So, the big question is, "Why did the miracle that you were able to see with your very own eyes actually happen?"

Before explaining **why**, we first would like to pause to make what we consider to be a very important point, and that is for us to highly honor your free will. What we mean by this is that as we explain why the miracle happened, followed by giving you ideas of what we think is really good to do in light of the explanation, we in no way want to have even a hint of sales manipulation. In other words, there are many times when someone will give you a sales pitch, and in that sales pitch they try to make it sound as though it is only for your benefit, when in reality their main motive is to try to manipulate you into buying what they want you to buy, so that they in turn can make money. Since sales manipulation is so prevalent, we would like to state up front our desire to not manipulate you in any way, but to simply state our explanation and recommendations, and to give you the complete freedom to choose what you would like to do with them – whether something or nothing. With this disclaimer in place, we now feel the freedom to continue with the explanation…

The reason the miracle occurred was because there is this very-much-more-than-we-can-realize incredible, wonderful, amazing, and invisible being who took the time and effort to grow the many things needed for the miracle to take place – such as bone, tissue, etc.

So, the next big question is, "Why did this amazing being actually do this miracle **for you**?"

The reason this being did this miracle on your behalf is so that you could know that this being actually exists, loves you and values you, and in this love and value desires your very best. In this context, the very best that this being can offer you is a close relationship of friendship with this being – first for your sake, not first for the sake of this being. And because this being has such tremendously selfless love for you, this being will not force friendship upon you, but allows you instead to go through the discovery process of coming to know that this being exists, desires a close friendship with you, and allows you the total free choice as to whether you would like to accept or reject that friendship offer.

So if you would like to accept this being's friendship offer to you, then you will probably want to know four things:

Thing 1: How can you be a friend with an invisible being?

Thing 2: Who is this being?

Thing 3: What is involved in such a friendship?

Thing 4: How does one accept the friendship offer?

If you would like to know about these four things, **feel free to read on…**

Thing 1: How can you be a friend with an invisible being?

To be a friend with this invisible being requires that you are able to know that this being actually exists, even if you cannot see this being with your eyes. It is like a blind person having friends, even though they cannot physically see those friends. The blind person has ways other than sight in which they can know and interact with those friends. And fortunately, this being is not only able to demonstrate that this being exists by invisibly working in the miracle you experienced, but this being can also give you the needed ability to know for sure that this being truly exists. This is similar to you walking into a dark room and turning on a light to be able to see what is in the room. So, this being is able to activate a light in you, so to speak, so that you can not only know the reality that this being actually exists, but you can also have a wonderful friendship with this being! Later on, we will explain more about how you can turn on this light by asking this invisible being to turn on the light for you.

As a side note, you may wonder why this being stays invisible most of the time. Part of the answer is that if this being showed up visibly, a person would be so overwhelmed by the greatness of this being, that it would make it harder for the person to go through the discovery process of finding this being and having the free choice as to whether they would like to accept or reject the friendship offer of this being.

Thing 2: Who is this being?

So, who is this being?

Since people can have very different definitions for the same word, we will first give you a further definition of this being before giving you the name of this being.

Some of the characteristics and desires of this being were described in an earlier paragraph. Here is a quote of that paragraph with some of those characteristics and desires emphasized in bold font.

> The reason this being did this miracle on your behalf is so that you could know that this being actually exists, **loves you and values you**, and in this love and value **desires your very**

best. In this context, the very best that this being can offer you is a close relationship of friendship with this being – first for your sake, not first for the sake of this being. And because this being **has such tremendously selfless love for you**, this being **will not force friendship upon you**, but allows you instead to go through the discovery process of coming to know that this being exists, **desires a close friendship with you**, and **allows you the total free choice** as to whether you would like to accept or reject that friendship offer.

So, we can see that this being has tremendous characteristics and desires. But it is even more than was just described. Here is an expanded list of these characteristics and desires:

~ This being is always perfect in motives.

~ This being values you tremendously.

~ This being is never partial and never commits an injustice.

~ This being never lies.

~ This being is incredibly knowledgeable and wise.

~ This being always has selfless love toward you.

~ This being always desires your very best.

~ This being always desires that you value yourself.

~ This being always desires that you would know that you are very significant.

~ This being knows you completely – even more than you know yourself.

~ This being never makes a mistake.

~ This being always desires that you would be freed up into the very best for your life.

~ This being's character and desires have always been consistently good, and will always continue to be so.

~ This being desires a close friendship with you – first for your sake, not first for the sake of this being – since this is the greatest gift that this being can give to you!

So, who is this being with such wonderful and amazing characteristics and desires?

This being goes by a name that I, Scott, used to not like because of the negative concepts I had associated with the name. But now, I really like the term "God" because I now see "God" as having all of these wonderful and amazing characteristics and desires.

So, realizing the term "God" may still have negative connotations for you, feel free to substitute a term such as "The Source of Love" or "The Amazing One" if that would work better for you – since "God" is just a label for the amazing being that we described earlier.

From this point forth we will refer to this being as God and also as He/Him/His, etc., even though God is gender neutral – having both male and female characteristics.

Thing 3: What is involved in such a friendship?

Many people think that God is trying to impose His will upon them in His wanting them to do things that are foreign to whom they truly are. And accordingly, they think that God just wants them to perform certain boring religious duties for some unknown reason. But, if we look at the last of the characteristics and desires listed earlier, we see:

~ This being desires a close friendship with you – first for your sake, not first for the sake of this being – since this is the greatest gift that this being can give to you!

If our starting place is friendship, then a whole different picture emerges. It is a picture of two close friends (you and God) growing in deeper friendship. And the more you discover about God, the more amazed you will be at how absolutely amazing and wonderful He is! And to enjoy and appreciate God is the most rewarding thing possible in this life and throughout eternity!

Not only do you get to grow in your enjoyment of God (which is by far the best thing in life now and through eternity), but you also get to join Him in a privileged partnership of friendship where you get to tag along with God in things that He is doing. More specifically, God has perfect love toward others, and as you hang out with Him, you will find that you will pick up on His love for others, and in turn you will have more love for them. In this, God's love will become the basis for you being able to love and value God, yourself, and others, since it is based upon His unchangeable perfect love and not upon other things that can so easily change – such as how your feelings might change when someone does something for you that you like, but in the next moment does something that you do not like. And growing in this consistent love provides a tremendous foundation for your friendships with others to flourish.

In addition to this, since God knows the future and is so much smarter than we can even begin to fathom, He knows the very best things for us to do in our friendship partnership with Him. And God offers this guidance to you as a gift if you are willing to use your free will to receive it. Once again, this is not God imposing this upon you, but freely offering it to you. In this, God will guide you sometimes through inspiration – where you will find yourself inspired to do something and then, as you do that thing, you will discover that it was God invisibly guiding you all along. At other times, it will be His direct guidance for you to do a certain thing with Him – even if at first you do not understand the value of doing that thing. But, as you follow His guidance, He will often teach you as you go with Him, and over time, you will get to see what He already knew was the very best before He gave you the initial guidance to go in such a direction.

It can be a lot of fun participating with God in what He is doing – even miracles such as legs growing out, miraculous instant healings, and more! And being able to see the positive effects upon others is a real treat as God gives you things to do that not only build great friendships, but also help others in great ways. For example, God may give you wise insights for you to offer to a person, such as something they can do that will help their marriage. And if that person looks to God to help them apply those insights, then you may get to enjoy seeing how it is so helpful to them, their spouse, and to any kids they might have. They in turn will most likely appreciate you being of help to them. And all of this can help in growing your friendship with them. Another example is that we have enjoyed partnering with God as He miraculously grows out people's legs, and if in turn they no longer have to deal with chronic back pain, then we are all the happier for them!

Even though there are so many wonderful aspects of being in a privileged partnership of friendship with God (even more than we have listed so far), there is also a very challenging part of friendship with God. And that is the trials and refining He will take you through so that you can be freed up and grow to be more like God in His wonderful friendship characteristics and desires. And through this growth, you will be able to participate better and more fully with God in the wonderful things that He is doing.

In our lives, we at times find the trials and refining to be a very challenging process, but also incredibly worthwhile, since through this process God grows us in relational abilities and characteristics that enable us to enjoy Him more and to be better friends to Him, others, and even ourselves. This is similar to the military taking a soldier through a grueling boot camp. At times the soldier may wonder if it is really worth it. But in the long run, the soldier will wind up being in great physical condition and much better equipped for the challenges of military life.

There are also challenges that may not seem obvious at first, in that there are demonic forces that hate God with all their being (which is a whole other story as to why), and because of your association with God, these demonic forces will hate and tempt you all the more. And they will tempt others to hate and be mean to you as well. But as you learn to forgive, love, and to be kind to such people by God's love and help, you will become all the more equipped and it will be all the easier for you to love and be a friend toward those who are much easier to deal with. So, although this aspect of life with God can be quite challenging at times, in the long run it will become clear that this process is incredibly worthwhile, and you will be eternally grateful for it!

Thing 4: How does one accept the friendship offer?

If you would like to enter into and participate in a privileged partnership of friendship with God that was previously described in the "Thing 3" section, then how can you actually do this?

First of all, you would need to be willing to commit your life to God for all of the things described in the "Thing 3" section, since these things are needed for your friendship with God to work well. So, if this is what you would like to do with your life and you are willing for these things, then **feel free to read on** for how to actually accept God's friendship offer to you…

Note: The following may be a little hard to understand at first (at least it was for us), but the more we learn about it, the more amazed we are at how wonderful it is! So, how can we explain it so that it is easy for you to understand? We will attempt to do so by first starting with the following metaphor.

Suppose you have a friendship with someone, and that person does something really mean to you that you thought was totally unjustified. What would be needed to restore your friendship with that person? Most likely the person would need to apologize to you and you would need to be willing to forgive them. Otherwise a relational barrier would still remain between the two of you.

In a similar way, all relational barriers between you and God would need to be removed in order for you to be able to enter into a privileged partnership of friendship with God.

So, you would need to be willing to apologize to God for anything you have done against Him. And since God has given everyone their existence, you would also need to be willing to apologize to God for anything you have done against others and even against yourself – since such things indirectly go against God as well.

So, if you are willing to say to God something like:

> Please forgive me for all of the things that I have ever done against You, others, and even myself. I am sorry I did them in the first place, and I look to You to help me to avoid such things in the future.

Then will God forgive you and remove all of the relational barriers between you and Him?

We can find the key to answering this question by looking at the leg growing miracle. Why did the key name of Jesus work, but all of the other names did not work? What this shows us is that there is something very significant about the name of Jesus. Not only is the name of Jesus key for the leg growing miracle, but it also holds the key for you being able to truly receive forgiveness from God and to come into a close friendship with Him. So, if we can first understand who Jesus is and what Jesus did for us, it is the key that we need.

Jesus lived on earth over 2,000 years ago and was both ordinary and extraordinary. Jesus was ordinary in that He was very down-to-earth, relational, and approachable. Jesus was incredibly extraordinary in that He had the fullness of God dwelling in Him. In other words, God did an incredibly amazing thing by coming down to earth as a human – taking on both human characteristics and also characteristics unique to God. In Jesus' humanness, He got hungry and tired, felt pain, and experienced normal human emotions. In His divine nature, Jesus had all of the amazing characteristics and desires of God that we looked at earlier.

And the amazing thing Jesus did for you was something He really did not want to do because of how painful and ugly it would be. Much worse than having to do chores that He did not feel like doing. Much worse than having to go to a job that He did not feel like going to. Instead, it was sacrificing His very life to pay for all the things humans have done that have worked against them being able to love God, others, and themselves. This was not only for humans of that day, but for all humans: past, present, and future.

Side note: From this point forward, we will use the term "relational violations" to represent all of the things humans do that work against them being able to love God, others, and themselves. This even includes things that are not easily seen as working against someone being able to love God, others, and themselves, but in reality are things that actually do so and in turn contribute toward the forming of relational barriers.

What had occurred was that the government of Jesus' day thought they were simply executing Jesus to please the religious people who had wanted Jesus to be killed. Those people did not like Jesus doing many miracles and promoting relational friendship that in turn made them look bad in their non-relational religiousness. They were also jealous of Jesus' popularity. On top of this, Jesus claimed to be God – which those people considered to be blasphemous (in other words, a really bad thing to do in their view). Because of all of this, they persuaded the government officials to have Jesus executed through crucifixion – which is a slow death by hanging on a cross (a much nastier version of modern day lethal injection or even a firing squad). So, from their perspective they wanted Jesus out of their lives permanently, but from God's perspective He allowed this sequence of events to play out so that He could give an incredible example of the kind of love that He has for you, and for all humans, by providing a means of forgiveness based upon His paying for all of our relational violations on the cross. And after Jesus died, He then did another amazing thing by rising from the dead! Death could not hold Him since He was indeed God and also flawless in that He had never committed a relational violation Himself. His resurrection shows that God's payment for us on the cross is complete! It is paid in full, so to speak!

The crucifixion of Jesus can seem a little strange at first if we do not realize it is God Himself paying for all of the relational violations. In other words, it is not like a parent (God) who beats up their child (Jesus) so that they can be kind to the other kids in the neighborhood (us) on behalf of that beat up child. If such were the case, we would most likely conclude that God is not truly loving. So it was not just Jesus as a human taking on physical punishment, instead it was the huge heart of God taking on all the relational violations that all humans have done toward each other and toward Him. Our guess is that the heart of God is probably much bigger than at least from the earth to the moon, since God Himself is larger than our universe and even larger than we can comprehend. And that huge heart of God was filled with pain as it took on all of the pain of all relational violations. The thought of doing this for just one person is amazing let alone for all people of all times! So this was an amazing demonstration and sample of the kind of love that God has for you!

The cross establishes an anchor for how loving God is toward you and can help you to understand certain questions such as, "Is God a distant God or does He truly love me and care that I have to deal with the challenges of life?" The cross shows you that God has a tremendous heart of love for you and is willing to suffer more on your behalf than any suffering that you will face in life. With the same kind of love God had for you when He hung on the cross and paid for all of your relational violations, He is willing to walk through life with you and to help you with all of the challenges that you go through. So, if you are willing to commit your life to God, and receive His love and forgiveness according to His payment for you on the cross, then He is willing to forgive you and to even come and live inside of you through His Holy Spirit – and then to help you from the inside! For God to be willing to be so close to you that He is willing to live inside of you by His Spirit is incredible! Instead of you having to live like an orphan out on your own, God is willing to adopt you into His family – under His wings, so to speak! Instead of abandoning you, God is willing to always be with you – even with you through any suffering that you wind up going through. So, if you understand that God loves you that much and He is inviting you into a wonderful privileged partnership of friendship with Himself, and you are willing to put that friendship as a top priority so that He can free you into all that He knows you are uniquely designed to be and to become, then God's work on the cross on your behalf is the needed key for you to access all of this.

So putting all of this together, here are steps you can take to have all of the relational barriers removed between you and God and to come into a close friendship with Him. You could say the following to God out loud or in your heart/mind:

> I commit my life to You for all of the things described in the 'Thing 3' section, since these things are needed for a privileged partnership of friendship with You to work well. I am sorry for all of the relational violations I have made toward You, others, and myself. I look to You to help me to avoid such violations in the future. I ask You to forgive me according to Your payment for me on the cross. Please fill me with a great measure of You (Your Holy Spirit) and please help me to become a wonderful friend to You as I join You in a privileged partnership of friendship. According to the name of Jesus I ask You for these things. Thank You!

What an amazing step you just took! It is even more amazing than the miracle of your leg growing out!

Now that you have taken this amazing step, you may wonder if there is anything that can help you to do well in your friendship with God. There are two things that we would highly recommend.

The first thing is in regard to what we had shared with you earlier, when we said:

> So, this being is able to activate a light in you, so to speak, so that you can not only know the reality that this being actually exists, but you can also have a wonderful friendship with this being! Later on we will explain more about how you can turn on this light by asking this invisible being to turn on the light for you.

So now that you have already asked God to forgive you and to fill you with His Holy Spirit, we would recommend that you say the following to God out loud or in your heart/mind:

> God, please turn on the light, so to speak, so that I can know the reality of Your existence. And in this, please give me an incredible knowledge of Your presence with me. According to the name of Jesus, I ask this of You. Thank You.

We think it is incredible that God can enable us to know His presence and to grow us in a great friendship with Him. And we find that asking Him for such things is really helpful to do.

The second thing we would highly recommend is that you would read the fairly short **Deeper Friendships** which we are providing free of charge for you at **www.DeeperFriendships.com**. It builds upon **Would you like to see an Amazing Miracle?** and gives additional details in what we have found to be very helpful in a life of friendship with God.

We hope you have enjoyed reading ***Would you like to see an Amazing Miracle?*** and have enjoyed seeing at least one miracle! And we also hope it has helped you toward the greatest treasure of living a life of friendship with God!

Warmest regards,

Scott and Bonna Brooks

Deeper Friendships

Practical insights toward
wonderful friendships with
God and each other

Scott Brooks

Deeper Friendships

By Scott Brooks

www.DeeperFriendships.com

Practical insights toward wonderful friendships with God and each other

ISBN 978-1-6230946-2-1

Please note: If you have not yet read *Would you like to see an Amazing Miracle?*, you may want to first do so before reading *Deeper Friendships*, since *Deeper Friendships* builds upon it. You can read *Would you like to see an Amazing Miracle?* for free at: **www.SeeMiracle.com**

Table of Contents for Book 3 – *Deeper Friendships*

Dedication

I dedicate this book to Jesus, who is the Author of Friendship!

I secondly dedicate this book to three really close friends of mine: My wife, Bonna, and my two children, Ann and David!

Introduction

As I walked down the sidewalk on that dark, damp night, the wet coldness cut through my clothes, giving me a chill to the bone.

An occasional person hurried past me without even a glance.

The street lights were few and far between, mostly lighting up the sidewalk and revealing the silhouettes of those seemingly lifeless buildings that only showed an occasional dim light from their inner recesses.

After walking a few blocks, I approached a building that looked much different from the others because of the amount of light that it poured forth onto the sidewalk and street in front of it.

When I got to the building, I peered through a window and saw quite a number of people. A few of them were walking from one place to another, but most of them were sitting at tables.

At first glance, the people seemed friendly – many with warm smiles on their faces.

At the back of the room, there was a large hearth with a splendid fire. By now, I was quite chilled, and also a bit hungry. I knew the hearth would do well in warming my body, and I thought maybe I could even get a bite to eat. So, I decided to venture inside.

As I pulled open the door, I noticed many coats hung up in a fair sized room in front of me, and to my right was the large room that I had seen from the sidewalk.

I was surprised that there was not a registration desk or a sign that said, "Please Seat Yourself."

I was not sure if I could trust the people, so instead of hanging up my coat, I only unzipped it to allow the warm air in. I then started walking slowly toward the large hearth, knowing that the air would be even warmer there.

In front of the hearth was a large table where most of the people had gathered. It looked as if people had taken empty chairs from adjacent tables in order to be part of this larger group.

Before I could make my way around the table to get closer to the hearth, I saw a man stand up from the far side of the table. He looked at me, and then proceeded to walk around the table toward me. I stopped to see if he was going to say something to me. I was hoping he was not going to ask me to leave. To my relief, he warmly greeted me, identified himself as Jesus, and asked if I would like to join him and the others at the table – indicating that the empty chair in front of me was mine to use if I so desired.

What struck me about Jesus' invitation was that I felt completely free to accept or reject his offer. As I later reflected upon his invitation, it eventually dawned on me that part of the freedom I felt was the lack of pressure, manipulation, or control that often had accompanied invitations that others had given me in the past. And I did not feel in any way that Jesus was subtly trying to make me feel bad about myself if I had decided to decline his offer.

*** This story is continued in the next chapter. ***

Wow! What a tremendous privilege! Can you imagine being invited by Jesus to join Him at His table? How would you feel about such an offer?

I would count it a privilege to be invited to join the table of a president or head of a nation. But how much greater a privilege to be invited by Jesus, who is the image of the invisible God and the Creator of the universe! The One to whom I owe my very existence! The One whose greatness no one can fathom! The One who is so great that He has to stoop down to just look upon the earth, let alone interact with those on the earth… and yet He does so in His perfect love for us! (See John 1:1-3, Psalm 145:3,113:4-6.)

Just to sit at His table would be amazing, let alone be a fellow participant with Him and those with Him!

Similar to this metaphorical story, in real life Jesus literally invites you and me to join Him in a wonderful friendship, where Jesus will help us to grow toward deeper friendships with Him and others as well!

I realize that only God can truly grow us toward these deeper friendships. I therefore encourage you before reading on, to first ask God to teach you and cause things to stand out to your heart, so that He can uniquely tailor this book to you as part of His very best for your life.

I want to be a true friend to you as I write this book. So, I do not want to impose upon you, or teach at you. Instead, I plan to just share my heart with you as if we were sitting in the same room together. And I welcome you to take those things that seem to touch your heart and resonate with the core of your being. I have already "road tested" many of the concepts in this book by sharing them verbally with a number of people. It has been very exciting seeing how God has worked through this material to help those people toward deeper friendships with Him and others!

This book starts the journey toward deeper friendships which is then continued in a book I wrote at an earlier date titled, *At His Feet*.

At His Feet has many practical insights in how to learn from God and grow in deeper friendship with God. Both of these are keys to our being able to grow in friendship with each other.

One of the points I share in *At His Feet* in a section titled, "How to grow in friendship with God," is how I have found it helpful in my friendship with God to focus on Jesus, since He is God and my personal point of contact with an infinite God. So in this book, I will refer to God mostly by the term Jesus – especially when I am speaking in regard to friendship topics. In saying this, I am not speaking against someone who finds it easier to relate to God as "God" or as the "Father" or even as the "Holy Spirit", since I am happy for them if their life with God works well with any of these focuses. I am only saying that focusing on Jesus works better for me, and therefore it will be easier for me to share from this perspective.

My desire is that Jesus will work through the words of this book to help each of us to grow toward deeper friendships with Him and each other. I hope you are encouraged and find some freeing thoughts that are helpful to you in your journey with Him.

---

* Note: In the story that starts this introduction and continues in the next chapter, I used lower case "h" when referring to Jesus as him, his, he, etc. But, in the rest of the book I will use an upper case "H", since He is God and I like to denote this distinction in this way. In the story, the narrator does not yet know who Jesus truly is, so the narrator would naturally write about Jesus with the lower case "h".

Chapter 1 – Life at Jesus' Table

I decided to accept Jesus' invitation, pulled up the chair he had offered me, and joined him and the others at the table.

The next few hours flew by as I became increasingly fascinated at the things that were happening at the table. Every once in a while I looked at the clock on the wall next to the fireplace, and was surprised at how much time had slipped by without me realizing it.

When I had first joined the table, I was happy that the people welcomed me. I was also glad that they invited me to freely partake of the food at the center of the table, since the aroma had stirred my hunger all the more. I found it to be quite tasty and satisfying.

As my hunger subsided, I began to observe a number of very fascinating things. For starters, I was quite impressed at how the people treated each other. I was surprised that there were no arguments, and they did not seem to be competing or trying to outdo each other. Instead, they genuinely seemed to care for each other, demonstrating this in many ways, such as how they were respectful and patient with each other. One person had a stutter and other people did not seem impatient or try to pressure the person to speak more quickly. And instead of superficial conversations, most of the people seemed to share deeply from their hearts, and also listened intently to the others. I could tell they were listening well by the clarifying questions they asked to those speaking, and also by the way the conversation rolled along so nicely. I was especially amazed to see someone stop speaking in mid-thought to allow someone else to share, because that other person seemed to have something more pressing on their heart to share than they did. And this did not happen just once, but a number of times throughout the evening.

Sometimes there was one large conversation. Other times discussion split into multiple smaller conversations. I thought it was especially interesting at the times when Jesus spoke. When there was only one conversation, people seemed to hang on every one of his words. When there were multiple conversations, people seemed to bend an ear toward Jesus from those other conversations. This sometimes resulted in those other conversations joining the conversation that Jesus was part of.

More chairs were positioned near Jesus than by anyone else at the table. I assumed most of these chairs were those that had been borrowed from the adjacent tables. At first I thought it was a bit odd that people were leaning toward Jesus, and occasionally even nudging their chairs closer to him. But, as the night went on, I began to realize that the people seemed attracted to the warmth and care Jesus showed to each of them. His example also seemed to set the tone for how they were treating each other. Overall, I was really struck by how everyone seemed to feel valued and have a strong sense of well-being, and how they seemed to enjoy just being with Jesus and each other. It was as if there was an "otherness" to the whole atmosphere. This was a great contrast to the tensions I had seen in so many relationships – including my own.

I eventually became quite curious to know if my observations were close to the mark, and to also know what things I had overlooked. So, I turned to the older gentleman on my right – who seemed to have shared a few insightful things during the evening – and I said, "I think it is pretty amazing, some of the interactions I am seeing at this table." I proceeded to share some of my observations, and then asked him what his thoughts were. He then said…

"Whenever Jesus comes to town, I love to go to wherever he is. There is not anyone whom I would rather be with than Jesus! He avoids the ugliness that appears in cliques or when people compete with each other to the point where they become nasty, and instead he shows great love and value to people. It is great to see how others enjoy being loved and valued by him, and I am glad to be a recipient of his love as well. The amazing thing is that, without even a word, others feel the love Jesus has for them. You can see the twinkle in his eyes, but it is more than that – it is as if his whole being has love flowing through it! I have noticed small kids and animals are especially drawn to his love for them. But some older people respond well too, such as those at this table. And when Jesus does speak, he speaks to the heart of the individual. So, the thing I love most about being here at this table is just being with Jesus and watching him interact with others.

"It is also fun being with the other people who have gathered with Jesus – such as those at this table. We love to hear what each person shares from their heart. As they share, we listen intently and pay special attention to what stirs in our own hearts. It often pertains to our own lives or the lives of people we know, and by listening this way, it often provides the clue as to what is on our hearts to add to the conversation. As we share with each other in such a way, we enjoy the richness of the conversation, plus we all wind up being encouraged. And when people have shared burdens and things that have been troubling them, it is nice to listen to them and pray for them. I also appreciate seeing how others have followed the lead of Jesus and the seasoned table veterans, to not talk down to or lecture those people in struggle. Instead, they mostly share those things they have found to be of practical value in their own lives in those same or similar areas.

"Through all of this I have marveled at how our friendships have grown. I highly value these people and count it a privilege to have such deep and precious friendships with them. It brings a quality to our lives that we would not have without our friendships with Jesus and each other.

"You would think that over the years I would begin to take some of this for granted. But especially in light of all of the bad relationships I have seen, I am still amazed at how Jesus has helped to free each of us up toward further places of friendship with him and each other.

"Oh, and one last thing… I think it is fun to observe newcomers, such as you, who join the table and try to piece together and understand how these deep friendships really work. I think it is great when these newcomers are inspired to go deeper toward quality friendships in their own lives."

I enjoyed the insights this man shared with me and realized there was a quality of life these people had found that I myself was lacking, and it definitely whet my appetite to grow in these good ways myself.

As I listened to this man and to the conversations that evening, it started to dawn on me where I had failed in my own relationships. I tentatively concluded that the discussion at this table tonight and on future nights could really help me to become a better husband and parent, and also help me in my work relationships. In fact, I could see it being helpful for all the relationships of my life!

At the end of the evening, I was very thankful Jesus had extended an invitation to me, and that I had the opportunity to be part of such an experience. I just could not get over how these people had such a sparkle in their eyes and seemed to appreciate and value each other in such a great way. It definitely was beautiful to see such interactions, and it whet my appetite for more. So, in the future, when Jesus comes to town, I definitely want to find the table where he is at and hang out there as much as possible!

***** **End of Story** *****

I just love this story! It paints a picture of a wonderful place for us all to grow toward – a place of deep, quality friendships with Jesus and each other, where there is a wonderful "otherness" of life that we will experience together.

Jesus Himself says that where two or three are gathered in His name, He is there with them. (See Matthew 18:20.) So although we can experience God's presence in our lives as individuals, God has designed things in such a way, that only together with others who are also in relationship with Him, will we experience His presence in a greater way. And what greater joy than being with Jesus! The following verses describe the joy we can experience together at this place.

> That which was from the beginning, which we have heard, which we have seen with our eyes, which we have looked at and our hands have touched—this we proclaim concerning the Word of life. The life appeared; we have seen it and testify to it, and we proclaim to you the eternal life, which was with the Father and has appeared to us. We proclaim to you what we have seen and heard, so that you also may have fellowship with us. And our fellowship is with the Father and with his Son, Jesus Christ. We write this to make **our joy complete**. (1 John 1:1-4, emphasis mine)

The Apostle John describes how he and others have experienced Jesus in person – they saw, heard, and touched Jesus! And in verse three, we can see that John invites his readers to join the deep, quality friendships (i.e. fellowship) that he and those other people have with Jesus.

> We proclaim to you what we have seen and heard, **so that you also may have fellowship with us. And our fellowship is with the Father and with his Son, Jesus Christ.** (1 John 1:3, emphasis mine)

I find it quite interesting why John says he is writing to his readers.

> We write this to make **our joy complete**. (1 John 1:4, emphasis mine)

If John was being selfish, he may have said, "**my** joy complete." But, instead he says, "**our** joy complete." Since John hung out with Jesus, it is no surprise that Jesus helped John to love others. And as John had God's love for the people he was writing to, he wanted them to experience the joy found when all together, they could experience deep friendships with Jesus and each other. It is a small taste of heaven, for in heaven there will be a wonderful sense of well-being and joy as we will finally know and experience Jesus completely! And together with Jesus we will experience being completely loved, have complete intimacy of heart, and know each other completely. On top of all this, we will get to marvel at how awesome and wonderful God truly is all the time, as we see Jesus face to face!

This is a lot nicer than what happens in many relationships where people try to win at the expense of others losing. Instead, as we grow toward deeper friendships with Jesus and each other, it will be good and pleasant, and we will all win together!

> How **good and pleasant** it is when brothers live together in unity! It is like precious oil poured on the head, running down on the beard, running down on Aaron's beard, down upon the collar of his robes. It is as if the dew of Hermon were falling on Mount Zion. For there the LORD bestows his blessing, even life forevermore. (Psalm 133, emphasis mine)

But if we fail to grow toward deeper friendships, we will miss out on so much! On the surface, our lives may look like we are doing good things, but in reality we will be lacking the relational qualities described in the story that began this chapter. The following verses give a strong example of this.

> Not everyone who says to me, 'Lord, Lord,' will enter the kingdom of heaven, but only he who does the will of my Father who is in heaven. Many will say to me on that day, '**Lord, Lord, did we not prophesy in your name, and in your name drive out demons and perform many miracles?**' Then I will tell them plainly, '**I never knew you. Away from me, you evildoers!**' (Matthew 7:21-23, emphasis mine)

At the Day of Judgment, when Jesus evaluates a person from His

DEEPER FRIENDSHIPS | 147

perfect perspective, it will become very clear if they truly knew Him or not. And "knowing" is an indication of deeper friendship. So if we never grow toward deeper friendships, we can do many seemingly good things, and yet never experience the joy of being with Jesus and each other.

But if someone is growing toward deeper friendships with Jesus and others, they will most likely want to continue to grow in such excellent ways. For example, if a teenager in their rebellious years is growing toward these deeper friendships, then when they get older, they will most likely stay walking with God and continue to be attracted to healthy and deep friendships – even if they eventually leave their parents' household to go on to other things such as to college or a job at a different location. But, if they are unable to grow toward these deeper friendships, then they may externally conform to their parents' expectations, but still feel relationally isolated. And since they were not better connected in their hearts, then as they grow older, they will be more likely to walk away from any connection they felt toward God and move toward unhealthy and hurtful relationships.

So, the big question is, "Can we actually grow toward this wonderful place of deeper friendships with Jesus and each other?"

Fortunately, the answer to this question is, "Yes, with Jesus' help"… **but**, with the qualification that there will be many challenges in growing in this excellent direction. We can see this in the following verses.

> **"I tell you the truth," Jesus replied**, "no one who has left home or brothers or sisters or mother or father or children or fields **for me** and the gospel will fail to **receive a hundred times as much in this present age (homes, brothers, sisters, mothers, children and fields—and with them, persecutions**) and in the age to come, eternal life. But many who are first will be last, and the last first." (Mark 10:29-31, emphasis mine)

If a person allows Jesus to help them on toward deeper friendships, then they will receive much more relationally in terms of "brothers, sisters, mothers, children" … but also persecutions (i.e. challenges).

Summary

In this chapter we concluded the story about the friendships at Jesus' table, with a more detailed look at the quality of the friendships being experienced there. We also looked at some of the pros and cons of growing or not growing toward such friendships, and overall seeing that it is of great value to grow in such ways – and yet, it will have its challenges.

Chapter 2 – A High-Level Overview

A new homeowner found an old garden hose in the back yard under the bushes. As he reached to pull the garden hose out, the idea crossed his mind that it would be nice to use the hose to water the garden, since he was a new homeowner and had not purchased a hose yet. As he pulled the hose out, he realized it was pretty beat up and in need of repair – most noticeable were the gashes that would surely leak. He realized he could just buy a new hose, but for some reason he took a liking to this particular hose and decided to repair it instead. He proceeded to replace the washer so that it could seal well to the outdoor faucet, and he also repaired the gashes so that they would not leak. He then hooked it up to the faucet, turned the valve counterclockwise, and began to spray water onto the garden. Over time a wonderful crop of fruits and vegetables came forth from the garden – fresh tomatoes, green beans, strawberries, and all kinds of good things to eat.

Contained within this metaphor are many insights about deeper friendships with Jesus and each other. We will explore the details of these insights in the chapters that follow this one, but for now let us take a high-level overview of this metaphor's basic components.

> ~ The garden hose represents a person, whether you, or me, or someone else.

> ~ The water that flows through the hose is God – in the reservoir as God the Father, and through the hose as God the Holy Spirit.

> ~ The homeowner, who does the gardening, is also God but in the person of Jesus.

> ~ The hose getting repaired and hooked up to the house represents a person coming into a relationship with God.

~ The fruits and vegetables in the garden represent the good results that grow in the person's relationships with Jesus and others.

Most metaphors break down at a certain point since they do not perfectly describe reality. So is the case for this garden hose metaphor. For one thing, we are much more than a hose in that we have a brain, heart, soul, spirit, and unique personalities. Secondly, growth toward deeper friendships is much more complex and challenging than the restoration steps needed for the garden hose. Also, the garden hose does not have the free will that we do. We can choose whether or not we will allow the Gardener to repair us, hook us up to the faucet, and enable us to become useful over time in producing a garden harvest of deep friendships. Lastly, we have the thinking ability to evaluate the restoration process itself, but depending on how we perceive it, we may think it is better to move toward or keep away from such a restoration. So, if we do not understand why Jesus would want us to grow toward deeper friendships (which we will explore in the next chapter), and conclude it is better to just do our "own thing", then we can use our free will to choose the tragic results found in a dream that a friend of mine had.

Matt Scott's Dream

I was walking through the woods and came to a clearing at the edge of a very large and beautiful lake with glistening dark water. I was excited because I love to fish and was hoping the lake would prove to be excellent for fishing.

Jesus met me at the edge of the lake and took my hand. He then guided me to the water's edge. I started to wonder if we were going to walk on the water, since I knew Jesus had done so before. But instead, we began to walk into the water that initially was only up to our ankles. We walked further into the lake, but the water did not get deeper like I thought it would, instead it remained only ankle deep. We walked and walked and walked, but as far as we went, the water still remained only ankle deep. I was surprised that the lake was not any deeper and concluded the fishing would not be good since it was so shallow.

Jesus then began to weep. I was surprised by His sadness. Jesus then turned to me and said that the lake represents His body, the church. He loves His church, but is deeply saddened by the lack of depth.

When Matt shared his dream with me, it dawned on me that the lake looks beautiful on the surface because of Jesus' perfect love for those who have entered into relationship with Him. But, the tragedy is the shallowness of the water that represents a lack of relational depth. Jesus' heart longs for people to be freed up toward these deeper waters of friendship, and He is saddened for them that they are not getting any deeper than the shallow waters. So, if we do not get repaired, hooked up well to the faucet, and over time increase in the amount of water flowing through us, then we will never be able to participate in these deeper waters of friendship with Jesus – nor with anyone else. We may even be surrounded by many people, and yet feel like an isolated island – never truly connecting with others at deeper levels. We may long for better relationships, but find that whatever we try, we wind up just never getting there.

Summary

In this chapter we looked at an overview of the garden hose metaphor. We will look at the details of this metaphor in the following chapters in order to help us grow past the shallow ankle deep relational waters described in Matt Scott's dream, and instead on toward the deeper waters of friendship with Jesus and each other.

Chapter 3 – Our Original Design

When the Gardener found the garden hose under the bushes, he realized it would not work well in its current condition, since without a good washer it would not seal well to the faucet and water would also escape through the gashes. In such a condition, the hose would work poorly and be of little use in watering the garden. Fortunately, the Gardener had knowledge of how a new hose would work and was able to apply that knowledge to the restoration of the hose. If the Gardener had lacked this knowledge, then the restoration process would have been much more difficult and the hose may have never been able to function again according to its original design.

The Gardener's knowledge of the hose's original design was very helpful to his restoration of the hose. In a similar way, Jesus understands our original design, since He is the one who designed us! Fortunately, Jesus also knows all that is needed for us to grow toward functioning according to our original design! How we got to the state of being under the bushes in the first place is another matter that we will explore in the next chapter. But for this chapter, we will take a look at our original design, since if we can increase in an understanding of our original design, it will be one of the keys to our growing toward the deeper waters of friendship with Jesus and each other.

Interestingly, if the garden hose had intelligence like we do, but only knew what life was like under the bushes, then when the Gardener worked at restoring the hose to its original design, it may have wondered why the Gardener was doing such a thing – especially since the hose would begin to experience things that looked different from life under the bushes.

This raises the question of, "What is normal?" If the garden hose only knew life under the bushes, it would think such a life was normal. So if it left the shade of the bushes, was stretched out instead of being coiled, went through the repair process, was hooked up to the faucet, and had the water running through it, then it might conclude that this all seemed quite abnormal to its normal existence.

In a similar way, if we do not understand how we were originally designed to function and also why Jesus would want to restore us to that design, then it might seem abnormal to us. We might even conclude that God is trying to impose something upon us that is foreign to whom we really are, and therefore decide that we want nothing to do with it at all. So, for the rest of this chapter, we will explore two main concepts – the first concept being how we are designed to function, followed by the second concept of why Jesus would want to restore us to that design. Hopefully, with this groundwork in place, the subsequent chapters will then make a lot more sense and help us all grow toward the deeper waters of friendship with Jesus and each other.

How we are Designed

As we look at how God originally designed us to function, there are two extremes that if either is embraced will make it difficult to grow toward the deeper waters of friendship.

The one extreme is that we would function independently from God, just like the garden hose being under the bushes and away from the Gardener.

The other extreme is where we are taken over by God and cease to exist as an individual – much like a drop of water joining an ocean.

Between these two extremes is where our true design rests – at a partnership of deep friendship with Jesus.

A helpful question at this point is, "What do we bring to our partnership of friendship with Jesus, and what does Jesus bring?"

On our side of the partnership, we bring our spiritual hearts, souls, minds, and unique personalities that make us very much more unique than the unique fingerprints on our hands. We also have the ability to think, reason, interact, and more. All of these things are gifts from God, since if He did not exist and decide to create us, then we would not exist. So, our very existence is a gift from God to us, and we bring this unique existence to our partnership with Him.

If we enter into a friendship with Jesus – which we will look at the details of how to do in two chapters from now – then on Jesus' side of the partnership, He brings many things out of His great love for us. For starters, Jesus brings His Holy Spirit to flow through us like the water flowing through the garden hose. Over time, this in turn produces what is known as the "fruit of the Spirit" which is listed in Galatians 5:22-23 as: "love, joy, peace, patience, kindness, goodness, faithfulness, gentleness, and self-control." In addition to this, the Holy Spirit within us will also enhance our common sense and thinking by giving us insights into the various information coming into our senses – even insights needed to help us recognize what would be good to embrace or avoid if we are going to allow Him to help us to grow toward deeper friendships with Him and others.

Side note: Chapter three in **At His Feet** gives greater detail into how God can enhance our senses and teach us through this process.

It is a tremendous privilege to partner with Jesus in a deep, mutually respectful friendship. Not only do we get to participate in that friendship out of our free will, but we also get the amazing gift of partnering with Jesus in those things that are dear to His heart. To begin with, He has more love for others than we do and He allows us to join Him in having that love also. So, when His love begins to flow through us, we then grow in our love for Him, ourselves, and others. This love in turn gives us a tremendous basis for valuing Him, ourselves, and others. And the more we operate this way, the more it resonates with who we really are, since we are designed to live a life of love. (See Ephesians 5:1-2.) This goes right along with the two greatest commandments which are to love God, and to love our neighbors as ourselves. (See Mark 12:28-31.) In the context of partnership, it shows that these two commandments are not imposed upon us as abnormal to whom we are, but instead are a great freedom for us to participate with God's love as normal to our true design. And our design is to live a life of love and to partner with Jesus in doing the good things that we are uniquely designed for. As it says in Ephesians 2:10, "For we are God's workmanship, created in Christ Jesus to do good works, which God prepared in advance for us to do." This is a gift from Jesus to us, in that He will grow us into who we truly are as we learn to walk with His love flowing through us and as we partner with Him in doing the "good works" that are places where we can express that love, and where our friendships with Jesus and others can blossom.

And this partnership is a two-way street. Not only do we get to participate with Jesus according to our true design, but Jesus also participates with us in such things as what may be troubling us in our lives. For example, the following two scriptures show that in our friendship with Jesus, He is willing to give us both help and peace with our concerns.

> Cast all your anxiety on him because he cares for you. (1 Peter 5:7)

> Do not be anxious about anything, but in everything, by prayer and petition, with thanksgiving, present your requests to God. And the peace of God, which transcends all understanding, will guard your hearts and your minds in Christ Jesus. (Philippians 4:6-8)

Three more Metaphors

Similar to the garden hose metaphor, there are three additional metaphors that I find helpful in understanding how we are designed for such a partnership with Jesus.

The first metaphor is from John 15, where Jesus says He is like a

Vine and we are like the branches coming off the Vine. Jesus further says that if we remain in Him and He remains in us, then we will produce much fruit, but apart from Him we can do nothing – just as the branch apart from the Vine cannot produce fruit by itself.

The second metaphor is that of us being like a radio and God being like the radio signal. If the radio has a broken antenna, then it will not be able to pick up the signal and will only produce white noise at best. But if the antenna is repaired, then it can receive the signal well and play beautiful music. We are designed to play beautiful music from the signal of God's Spirit through us.

The third metaphor is that of us being like a lamp on a table and God being like the electricity. The lamp might look nice with its design, color, and shape, and yet, if the electricity does not flow through the lamp, it will never function well as it is designed to function. Someone might enjoy it as a decoration, but will not find it very useful for reading at night.

All three of these metaphors show that only when both parts are partnered together does the final result function as it was designed.

What is Love?

Before leaving this section on **how** we are designed, and moving on to the section about **why** Jesus would want these things for us, I would like to pause here and emphasize and explore a key point in all of this, and that is, "What is love?" This question is not only at the heart of this chapter, but at the heart of this entire book as well. So, let us explore this question of, "What is love?"

Some people say that love is an action and if you do something that looks loving, therefore it must be loving. But according to the scripture, love is listed as the first fruit of God's Holy Spirit and is also the very essence of God's character – as it says in 1 John 4:16, "God is love." In the hose metaphor we can see this in action as love comes from God and can flow through us back to God, to ourselves, and to others – hence watering the garden. So, the hose metaphor therefore gives us a picture of how we are designed to love God, our neighbors, and ourselves, using God's love as the source.

Earlier we looked at John 15 where Jesus says that we can do nothing if we, as the branches, are apart from Him, as the Vine. Is this really true? Since Jesus never lies, we know it is therefore true. (See John 14:6.) But how does it practically apply to life?

Since Jesus has designed us, a person will still show forth hints of how he or she is designed, even if that person is apart from the Vine. For example, a parent apart from the Vine may still have extra care toward his or her child. Or apart from the Vine, a girlfriend and boyfriend may still taste of love toward each other. But, to truly have God's love flow through us is impossible without us being hooked up well to the source of that love. When someone says to another person, "Well, you do all kinds of things for me, but I just do not feel loved," it is most likely an indication that the person saying such a thing is not experiencing God's love flowing through that other person toward them. And since we are all designed to love God and love our neighbors as ourselves, that person realizes deep down that something is not right when others do not have God's love for them. When I was an atheist teenager, I wondered why the other kids did not love me more. Somehow I knew they were supposed to love me, even though I did not know anything about Jesus or my original design. I realize now that I had the blueprint of my original design deep inside of me in the very fabric of my being, and according to that blueprint, I knew it would have been right for those people to love me. Interestingly, I was less aware that it would have been right for me to love them, too – an indication that I was still not hooked up to the Vine, and therefore my selfish focus was much more upon myself than on others. This in turn made it harder for me to realize the lack of love that I had toward them.

I think our understanding of love in this context is very important, otherwise we could be surrounded by a hundred people who have God's love flowing through them and are at deeper levels of friendship, and yet find ourselves unable to participate. Without God's love flowing through us, we will not be able to give or receive His love well, and we as garden hoses will not bear much in terms of beautiful fruits and vegetables. Instead, the garden dirt will be dry, hard, and cracked and we will wonder why it is that way, since deep down we know there should be so much more.

Why Jesus would want this for us

Even if we have a good idea of **how** Jesus designed us to function, it does not mean we know **why** He designed us this way. If we misunderstand **why**, then we can easily draw many incorrect conclusions about so much else, which in turn will most likely keep us from growing toward deeper friendships. So, in this section we will explore the important question of, "Why would Jesus want us to function according to our original design?"

The short answer is that Jesus so completely loves us that He would like to give us the very best He can, which is deeper friendships of love where we would love God, and love our neighbors as ourselves. He loves us so amazingly, that out of that love He is willing to take tremendously great efforts to restore us to function this way. Jesus has no desire to take away our free will, demand that we be a certain way, or impose upon us or box us into something that is foreign to whom we really are. Instead He desires, for our benefit, to free us up and enable us to function more and more according to our original excellent design. This is a more amazing gift than we will ever be able to comprehend during our life on earth.

To explore the longer answer, it would be helpful to start with a look at who God is in terms of His desires and characteristics. We can then build upon this toward a fuller answer.

The following section is from *At His Feet*, where I summarized some of God's main desires and characteristics and said they were "derived from many Bible verses" and that "I have also found them to be consistent with my own personal experience with God and what I have experienced of reality." I included verses for the reader as a place to start if they were interested in learning more.

Some of God's Desires

~ He desires our best (Jeremiah 29:11).

~ He desires a close relationship with us (John 15:15; Matthew 23:37).

~ He desires for us to value ourselves, others, and God (Matthew 22:34-40).

~ He desires that we would know that we are significant, both at the present time and throughout eternity (John 13:1-5; Isaiah 49:15-16; Revelation 2:17; 3:12).

~ He desires that we would be set free into His very best for our lives (John 8:36; 10:10).

Some of God's Characteristics

It is easy to attribute human motives and characteristics to God. But there will always be an "Other-ness" to God— aspects of His character that no human could ever attain. Here is a list of such characteristics:

~ He always wants our best (Romans 8:28).

~ He is always perfect in His motives (Isaiah 55:8-9).

~ He infinitely values us (1 Peter 1:18-19; Romans 5:6-11).

~ He is never partial (Romans 2:11; 1 Peter 1:17).

~ He never commits injustice (2 Chronicles 19:7).

~ He never lies (Numbers 23:19; John 14:6).

~ He always has selfless love toward us (1 John 4:8; Jeremiah 31:3; Psalm 36:5-7).

~ He is infinitely knowledgeable and wise (Romans 11:33-36; Isaiah 40:28).

~ He knows us completely (Matthew 10:30; Psalm 139:1-18).

~ He never makes a mistake (2 Samuel 22:31; Deuteronomy 32:4).

~ His character and desires have always been and will always be consistent throughout eternity (Hebrews 13:8).

These lists point to the amazing qualities of God. We are so used to human frailties and how people treat each other in not the nicest ways, that it is hard to believe Jesus has zero bad motives, but instead He is always 100% perfect in motives – which is clearly stated in the following verse:

God is light; in him there is no darkness at all. (1 John 1:5b)

It is amazing to me that God loves us completely all the time and always wants our very best! This is quite a contrast to a very selfish person who does not care at all about the feelings of others and is mostly concerned with whether or not they are happy – such as how I was as a teenager. But, the more loving a person is, the more their eyes focus outside of themselves, which in turn increases how much they care for others. But with God, His love is so perfect that His eyes focus completely outside of Himself! In this context, Jesus' heart is first for our good and then secondly for what would be good for Him. If we think Jesus is first concerned for Himself, then we might easily conclude that He does not really want our best, but instead is like a parent trying to vicariously live through their child because they are first concerned with how that child reflects upon them and not first for the child's best. But with Jesus being perfect in love, His heart's desire is to give us the very best, no matter the cost to Himself. And the very best He can give us is to free us up toward deeper friendships with Him and each other. And if we use our free will to go along with His very best to free us up toward functioning according to our original design, then it gives Him pleasure. This is similar to the Gardener enjoying watching the garden grow. Jesus with perfect motives enjoys watching us grow spiritually and produce good fruit – and in this He is very glad for our sake!

This is similar to a person caring for someone else and getting them a very nice birthday gift. They buy it, put it in a box, wrap it up, and wait for the other person to open the present. If the other person receives the gift and is happy with it, then it gives pleasure to the giver of the gift. If the other person rejects the gift or hates it, then it would most likely sadden the gift giver since they would be sad that the other person did not enjoy the gift.

It is also like a parent whose child goes to jail for committing a certain crime. The parent might have hoped for all kinds of good things for the child, and yet had to bear the weight of the sadness of seeing the child's life having taken such bad turns. So if the parent really cared for the child, they would have pleasure in seeing the child freed out of jail and restored toward functioning in good ways – especially in the child's relationships.

In the following story from the book of Luke, we get a glimpse into this wonderful heart of love that God has toward each of us:

> Jesus continued: "There was a man who had two sons. The younger one said to his father, 'Father, give me my share of

the estate.' So he divided his property between them.

"Not long after that, the younger son got together all he had, set off for a distant country and there squandered his wealth in wild living. After he had spent everything, there was a severe famine in that whole country, and he began to be in need. So he went and hired himself out to a citizen of that country, who sent him to his fields to feed pigs. He longed to fill his stomach with the pods that the pigs were eating, but no one gave him anything.

"When he came to his senses, he said, 'How many of my father's hired men have food to spare, and here I am starving to death! I will set out and go back to my father and say to him: Father, I have sinned against heaven and against you. I am no longer worthy to be called your son; make me like one of your hired men.' So he got up and went to his father.

"But while he was still a long way off, his father saw him and was filled with compassion for him; he ran to his son, threw his arms around him and kissed him.

"The son said to him, 'Father, I have sinned against heaven and against you. I am no longer worthy to be called your son.'

"But the father said to his servants, 'Quick! Bring the best robe and put it on him. Put a ring on his finger and sandals on his feet. Bring the fattened calf and kill it. Let's have a feast and celebrate. For this son of mine was dead and is alive again; he was lost and is found.' So they began to celebrate.

"Meanwhile, the older son was in the field. When he came near the house, he heard music and dancing. So he called one of the servants and asked him what was going on. 'Your brother has come,' he replied, 'and your father has killed the fattened calf because he has him back safe and sound.'

"The older brother became angry and refused to go in. So his father went out and pleaded with him. But he answered his father, 'Look! All these years I've been slaving for you and never disobeyed your orders. Yet you never gave me even a young goat so I could celebrate with my friends. But when this son of yours who has squandered your property with prostitutes comes home, you kill the fattened calf for him!'

" 'My son,' the father said, 'you are always with me, and everything I have is yours. But we had to celebrate and be glad, because this brother of yours was dead and is alive again; he was lost and is found.' " (Luke 15:11-32)

In this story we can see how God is like the father who had a heart of love for both of his sons, and in his love for them, he wanted their best. I am sure his heart was saddened when the younger son left. But, we can see the father's selfless love in how he not only gave his son the freedom to leave, but also the finances to do so! And when the younger son returned to be able to function in ways that he was more designed to function, the father ran to him and rejoiced and celebrated out of great excitement for his son! The father also had love for the older son. He did not reject him because of his attitude, but kindly tried to help his son to get freed up to appreciate and participate in the wonderful thing that had just taken place with his brother.

There is one final point that I find helpful in realizing Jesus definitely wants our best first for us, not first for Him – and that is that Jesus does not need our friendship in any way. Before He created our world or any humans, He was totally complete in His own love and friendship with the Father and the Holy Spirit. So He had no need for us, but in His love, creativity, and infinite wisdom, He decided to give us our existence. So if someone thinks they are doing Jesus a big favor by moving toward a relationship with Him, then they most likely do not yet realize the perfect character and desires of Jesus and the tremendous privilege they are being invited to partake of. As it says in scripture:

> And he is not served by human hands, **as if he needed anything**, because he himself gives all men life and breath and everything else. (Acts 17:25, emphasis mine)

Therefore, it is an amazing gift that Jesus in His perfect love for us would offer to help us grow toward our original design for deeper friendships with Him and each other.

Summary

In this chapter we looked at our original design for a partnership of deep friendship with Jesus. We also explored the reasons why Jesus would like to restore us toward functioning according to that design. For Jesus to be willing to do this for us is an amazing gift for sure! A gift that comes from His magnificent and perfect love for us! In the next chapter we will explore how we wound up moving away from our original design in the first place.

Chapter 4 – Steps Away from Our Original Design

When the homeowner had found the garden hose under the bushes, he realized the hose was not in the same condition as when it was originally manufactured. Instead of being flexible, it was stiff. Instead of being whole, it had gashes that would leak. Without an explanation from the prior homeowners, the new homeowner may have wondered how the hose wound up being under the bushes in the first place.

When we looked at this metaphor in the last chapter, we explored how we are like the garden hose and how we were originally designed to function. But we deferred to this chapter the question of how the hose got under the bushes in the first place. So, in this chapter we will explore this question. We will also look at common ways people try to resolve the conflict of feeling like there should be more to life than they experience in their "normal" existence.

How the hose got under the bushes

To find the answer to the question of how the hose got under the bushes in the first place, we need to go way back in history to the beginning of mankind and look at the Biblical story of Adam and Eve in the Garden of Eden. A person may not believe this story was an actual historical event like I do, and yet if they look at it, they will find it gives an excellent description of the root problems of humanity and explains how the hose got under the bushes.

At a most basic level, Adam and Eve enjoyed a wonderful, deep friendship with God and each other. This was their normal existence.

When they were tempted to eat the fruit that God had told them not to eat, they began to distrust that God was perfect in motives, perfectly loved them, and only wanted their **very** best. Instead, they pulled back their hearts from God and in turn caused a tremendous and terrible break in their friendship with Him. In this, they moved away from a beautiful partnership of friendship with God – where they did meaningful things together in this friendship, such as tending the Garden of Eden – to instead moving toward being independent from God. In terms of the hose metaphor, they went from being hooked up to the faucet with the water of God flowing through them, to being removed and placed out into the yard under the bushes.

When Adam and Eve broke their friendship with God, they became spiritually diseased. And this spiritual disease not only affected them, but became a spiritual hereditary disease that has infected all humans down through the ages to our present time. (The only exception to this was Jesus, since He is the only human to also be fully God.) Because people are so used to this spiritual disease and the effects that it has, many think it is normal – even though it is abnormal to their original design.

There are a number of symptoms that people experience in this separated condition. First of all, they no longer have God's love flowing through them back to God, themselves, and others. And without that love, the basis for valuing God, others, and themselves is greatly decreased. This in turn works toward a downhill slide that can even result in their hating and being mean toward God, others, and even themselves.

Another symptom is that deep down, many people want better friendships, and yet find they cannot quite get there. They feel lonely not only when they are by themselves, but even if they are with many other people, since even among many others, they can still feel relationally isolated. Their loneliness is often more acute when they are not with anyone else, and this in turn can drive them toward being with others. And yet, when they are with others, the relational strains tend to drive them away from relationships back toward being alone. These two forces tend to balance out at a point, and yet in any given season a person may try "just one more time" to make relationships work. Others just decide that being a loner is the less hurtful way to go.

Overall, many people feel lonely, but do not know how to solve that loneliness by growing in deeper friendships with Jesus and others. And yet the blueprint of who they were originally designed to be is still in the fabric of their being. So, deep down they know there is something more to get to – yet they cannot quite seem to get there. It is like they have an itch on their body somewhere that they cannot quite locate. I have noticed four stages that people often go through in trying to find the itch.

Four Stages

The first stage is the totally selfish stage where a person is only concerned with themselves and their own needs. They try to buy things, experience things such as tastier food or thrills such as skydiving, try to be number one at something, try another romantic relationship, and much more. And yet, no matter what they purchase, accomplish, or experience, they only find temporary satisfaction. They often think the very next thing will bring the satisfaction they so strongly desire. And yet after they finally get the next thing and experience it for a while, it disappoints them since it did not provide the satisfaction they thought it would bring. A person in this stage can go from thing to thing to thing, and stay permanently stuck in this stage without ever being able to locate the itch.

Some people make it into the second stage when they discover a certain satisfaction in helping others. They might help to tutor a school student, help a person to move to a new residence, or just provide a listening ear to a troubled person. As the person helps others, they find that somehow they begin to feel a little better about themselves. As they focus on the needs of others, it helps them to get a little further away from the self-centeredness of the first stage. And yet, as much as they do things for others, they still deep down do not feel totally appreciated or valued. They can even get discouraged that their efforts are not appreciated more. And once again, as much as they try to help others, they still cannot find the itch.

Some people make it to the third stage when they realize there is a spiritual dimension of who they are, and begin to seek spiritual understanding and apply spiritual principles to their life. As the focus of their life moves toward spiritual things, they find that it resonates to a certain degree with something deep within them that their second stage efforts of helping others did not get to. And if they begin to look to a higher power, it can help them move further away from the self-centeredness of the first stage, since they begin to see the higher power at the center of the universe instead of themselves. And yet, this stage also has limits. As much as they try to grow in spiritual ways, they still find they are unable to reach what is deep in their hearts to get to. The itch is still not found.

The person makes it to the fourth stage when they, like the garden hose, get repaired and hooked up to the faucet. As the faucet opens, they begin to have the water of God's love flow through them, and over time God's love becomes a wonderful basis for them to love and value God, others, and even themselves. They begin to grow in their partnership of friendship with Jesus and find purposefulness in their deepening friendships with Him and others – as the garden begins to produce good fruits and vegetables. This all finally begins to resonate with the core of their being, since they begin to function according to their true normal design.

In the next chapter we will look at the details of how a person can get hooked up to the faucet and in turn make it into the fourth stage. But before moving on to that chapter, let us first take a look at one more issue, mainly the topic of, "What really is sin anyway?" For if we have a narrow view of what sin is, then it can hinder us from being freed up by Jesus into His very best for our lives. If instead, we can get a wider view of what sin is, it can greatly help us to want to avoid it, since we will see more clearly how it can really hinder us from growing toward those deeper waters of friendship with Jesus and each other.

What really is sin anyway?

When Jesus was once teaching about prayer, He said that it is good for us to ask God to forgive us of our sins in light of our forgiving others who have sinned against us. He then added:

> For if you forgive other people when **they sin against you**, your heavenly Father will also forgive you. But if you do not forgive others their sins, your Father will not forgive your sins. (Matthew 6:14-15, emphasis mine)

It is interesting that these verses show sin in the context of relationships. When Jesus says, "they sin against you", He is talking about sin in terms of what I call "relational violation". In other words, seeing sin in light of the negative impact it has upon friendships.

To see this further, if we look over the entire Bible at the topic of sin, it shows that the essence of sin is all the relational violations that humans do that work against them being able to love God, others, and themselves. This makes sense since the greatest two commandments are to love God and to love our neighbors as ourselves, and anything that would work against this would classify as sin. This even includes things that are not easily seen as working against someone being able to love God, others, and themselves, but in reality are things that actually do so and in turn can contribute to the forming of relational barriers that can greatly hinder deeper friendships.

A person might say that Adam and Eve sinned against God, and therefore God removed them from the Garden of Eden. At a very basic level, this is a true statement. But if we only look at this basic level, we can miss the bigger picture of what is going on.

If we instead focus upon sin in terms of relational violation, we can see that Adam and Eve did a great relational violation against loving God and each other. As their hearts pulled back from God, it greatly hindered their ability to have God's love flow through them as much as it had before, and over time it had a terrible impact upon their friendships with God and each other. Not only this, as they began to doubt the perfect character of God, they no longer fully accepted God as God and instead made a great substitution where they themselves began to move toward that central position best occupied by God. In this they became "too big for their britches" and gave birth to pride and arrogance, which have had terrible impact upon friendships ever since. In just one generation after Adam and Eve, we can already see a striking example of this decline in friendships when their one son intentionally killed their other son!

If we look at sin from this perspective, we can see why God would not like it, since in His perfect love for us, He wants our very best. And in light of this, it saddens him that sin hinders us from growing toward our original design for deep friendships. This is similar to the story in the last chapter about the parent whose child went to jail. The parent was very saddened by seeing the child's life detoured from all the good things that they desired for the child.

Instead of seeing sin in terms of relational violation, some people view it more from what I call a checklist mentality. They think that God has a list of things that He does not like, such as playing cards, dancing, or drinking caffeinated beverages. So they diligently live by the checklist, and yet often do things that harm their friendships without realizing it – such as looking down on, and even rejecting those who do not follow the same checklist. They can even hinder others from moving toward friendship with Jesus, since those being hindered might conclude that if God just wants them to follow a bunch of rules and is really not interested in their very best, then they do not want anything to do with God at all.

But if instead of a checklist mentality, we begin to see sin from its true relational context, then it can be of great help to us. So, if we realize that Jesus only wants our very best, we get hooked up to the faucet, and God's love begins to flow through us, then over time, Jesus will help to open our eyes so that we see with greater clarity the correlation between what we do and the positive or negative long-term effects that it has upon our friendships with Him and others. The following verses show this correlation.

> Anyone who claims to be in the light but hates his brother is still in the darkness. Whoever loves his brother lives in the light, and there is nothing in him to make him stumble. But whoever hates his brother is in the darkness and walks around in the darkness; he does not know where he is going, because the darkness has blinded him. (1 John 2:9-11)

It is a great benefit for us to see this correlation more clearly, since as we better understand what sin truly is, we will grow in a desire to avoid it and the negative effects that it has upon our friendships with Jesus and each other. It is a great kindness of Jesus to help us to see this correlation better, since without such sight, we could do damage to our relationships without even knowing how we damaged them – just as the 1 John 2:9-11 verses show how it is hard to see clearly in the dark. The more we see this correlation, the more we will want to avoid sin – not because it is on a checklist – but because we do not want to be unloving toward Jesus and others. As we grow this way, it will resonate deep inside of us as being very right and good, since it will be in harmony with our true design.

Summary

In this chapter we looked at how the garden hose went from its normal existence to its abnormal existence under the bushes due to a terrible break in the relationship between humans and God. In this we saw that the true essence of "sin" is relational violation, instead of the commonly held view of a checklist mentality that causes further relational violations. We also looked at the symptoms people experience in the condition of being under the bushes, such as loneliness and relational strains, and how they often go through four common stages to try to remedy these symptoms. In the next chapter we will look at the details of the fourth stage that shows how the hose can be restored, hooked up to the faucet, and begin to function according to its original design.

Chapter 5 – A Big Step toward Our Original Design

The Gardener pulled the garden hose out from under the bushes, fixed it up, and hooked it up to the faucet. He then turned the valve counterclockwise, and the water began to flow. At first the water did not look clear since dust, dirt, and cobwebs were being washed out. But then the crystal clear water came forth as the garden began to be watered. Over time, a beautiful crop of fruits and vegetables came forth.

In this chapter we will look at how each of us can get hooked up to God, just like the garden hose got hooked up to the outdoor faucet. You may already be hooked up, and if you are, I hope this chapter proves to be a reminder of how fortunate you are to already be so connected and possibly give you additional insights into this amazing privilege. If you are not already hooked up, may this chapter give you the needed explanation for how you, too, can get hooked up, which is a key step toward your being able to grow toward your original design for deeper friendships with Jesus and others.

A Disclaimer on the Context of this Chapter

As we will see later in this chapter, there is a decision that Jesus gives each of us as to whether we would like to get hooked up or not. He will not demand us or manipulate us to do so, even though out of His love for us, His heart's desire is to give us this amazing gift. In light of this, even though I will share with you concepts and steps that you can take to get hooked up, in no way do I want to do a relational violation of the 1 Corinthians 13 definition of love that says, "It does not demand its own way." (1 Corinthians 13:5 NLT) Instead, I desire to be respectful of you as I treat you as a good friend without pressuring, manipulating, or coercing you to also get hooked up. I am personally glad that years ago, I made the decision to get hooked up, and I think it is great that my friendships with Jesus and others are growing in such good ways. And even though I think this is the best decision others can make as well, I foremost want to give you the freedom to choose whether or not you would like to get hooked up. With this disclaimer in place, I now feel the freedom to continue with this chapter.

Hookup Basics Overview

In order for the garden hose to be restored and hooked up to the faucet, it required certain actions on the part of the Gardener and it also required willingness on the part of the hose. Now granted, a hose is an inanimate object that does not have a choice, but in our case, there is action needed both by Jesus as the Gardener as well as us as the garden hose. So, in the following section we will look at the actions needed by Jesus, followed by a section about the actions needed by us. We will then be able to build upon both of these sections to look at the actual hookup steps.

Understanding what is needed on God's part

God did an absolutely amazing thing for you and me in order to provide a way for us to get restored and hooked up. I do not fully grasp how amazing it truly is, but from what I currently understand, I will share with you.

Many people know the following Bible verse that summarizes what Jesus did for us:

> For God so loved the world that he gave his one and only Son (Jesus), that whoever believes in him shall not perish but have eternal life. (John 3:16)

In light of the concepts in this book about seeing sin as relational violation, here is my own fuller version of John 3:16 that expands upon this tremendous thing God has done for each of us:

> For God so greatly loved each and every individual person that He gave Himself in the person of Jesus and went to the cross

on our behalf, where He experienced and paid for each and every hurtful relational violation that every individual person has ever and will ever experience by what others have done or will do to them. God took all of this upon Himself so that we could experience healing of all of the relational violations that others have inflicted upon us, and also forgiveness for the relational violations we have inflicted upon others. God is not a distant God who does not know our pain. Instead, He is an amazing God who loves each of us so fully that on the cross He personally experienced the pain of every relational violation that we have had or will experience in the future. And through this amazing payment, God provides the means of forgiveness needed for each person to enter into a deep friendship with Him both now and for eternity. This gives us a wonderful example of the kind of love that God has for each and every one of us. So, Jesus is not a distant God, but One who has intimate firsthand knowledge of all of the relational violation pain we have suffered.

I can only imagine how much it physically hurt Jesus to be executed by crucifixion, but on top of this can you imagine experiencing the pain of every hurtful relational violation that every single person has or will experience? Jesus, out of tremendous love for each of us, took all of this pain upon Himself so that you and I could receive healing for our wounded hearts, and forgiveness for all the relational violations we have made against others. If you think of the times you have been hurt by others, can you imagine multiplying that pain by what all people in past, present, and future generations have had and will experience? I cannot begin to fathom the kind of love that Jesus perfectly maintained in providing such a payment for each of us. Jesus freely laid down His very life as a blood sacrifice for each and every one of us so that He could offer you and me the free gift of forgiveness and healing. In the garden hose metaphor, forgiveness and healing are part of the hose restoration process.

In looking at what Jesus did for each of us, the following question comes to my mind, "How could a person of normal human size take all the relational violations of every single person upon Himself?" If Jesus was only a person, then this could not be humanly possible, but the following verses give us a clue as to how this was truly accomplished:

> For God was pleased to have all his fullness dwell in him (Jesus), and through him to reconcile to himself all things, whether things on earth or things in heaven, by making peace through his blood, shed on the cross. (Colossians 1:19-20)

It was this larger-than-we-can-imagine God of the universe that through Jesus, was taking all of these relational violations upon Himself. If we think about the distance from here to the moon, it gives us a place to start in thinking about the size of God's heart – which is even much larger yet. This huge heart was literally experiencing all of the pain caused by the relational violations done by every human in the past, present, and future. A square mile of size might be needed for a single person who has caused a lot of relational violation over the course of their life. If we now multiply this by every human that ever lived, lives now, or will live in the future, we see that God made an amazing payment for everyone by taking all of this pain upon Himself. The heart of God was truly filled with pain as Jesus hung there on the cross, and this gives us a small glimpse into the kind of love that God has for each of us. If you think of a person living near you, can you imagine taking upon yourself all of their pain that they experienced through the relational violations that others have inflicted upon them, so that they could be healed of that pain? Would you be willing to carry around their pain so that they no longer had to carry it? It would definitely be their pain at your expense. Could you now imagine doing this for every person of all generations? And yet, this is exactly what God did on the cross!

In chapter three I said, "But, with Jesus being perfect in love, His heart's desire is to give us the very best, **no matter the cost to Himself**." What Jesus did on the cross demonstrates the last part of this quote. He paid a cost that is off the charts in terms of sacrificial love. On the cross Jesus had you and me held in His heart even though we were not yet alive at that time, but He looked through time and embraced each of us. John 15:13 says, "Greater love has no one than this, that he lay down his life for his friends." And this is truly what Jesus did for you and me!

Jesus' payment on the cross is even greater than what I have described so far! Not only did Jesus pay for the human to human relational violations, but Jesus also paid for every relational violation that people have done against themselves and have also done against God. For example, a person may have the relational violation of hatred in their heart toward others, themselves, and God. So, God's payment on the cross is for people of all times. And it accounts for every past, present, and future relational violation. This includes both the obvious and less obvious things that people do that work against the greatest two commandments of them loving God, others, and themselves. All of this adds up to an absolutely awesome thing that God has done on the cross on our behalf and is more amazing than my mind can even begin to comprehend!

Understanding what is needed on our part

In the prior section we saw that God in the person of Jesus did a tremendous amount on our behalf to make it possible for us to get restored and hooked up. But what about us, what do we need to do in order to be able to partake of all that Jesus did for us on the cross and to join Him in a partnership of friendship?

If you or I wanted to become an accomplished musician, and an expert music teacher graciously offered to give us an instrument, music books, lessons, and coaching all for free, would the teacher be glad for us if we took the instrument and music books but never practiced, never showed up for lessons, and never paid attention to their coaching? Would it be surprising that we did not progress well toward our original desire to become an accomplished musician?

In a similar way, Jesus perfectly loves us, and in this love He graciously and freely offers to forgive us for all the relational violations we have ever done (according to His payment for us on the cross), to fill us with His Holy Spirit, and to enable us, teach us, and grow us toward our original design of a partnership of friendship with Him as is stated in chapter 3:

> And our design is to live a life of love and to partner with Jesus in doing the good things that we are uniquely designed for. As it says in Ephesians 2:10, "For we are God's workmanship, created in Christ Jesus to do good works, which God prepared in advance for us to do." This is a gift from Jesus to us, in that He will grow us into who we truly are as we learn to walk with His love flowing through us and as we partner with Him in doing the "good works" that are places where we can express that love, and where our friendships with Jesus and others can blossom.

If we only desire to be forgiven, but do not truly want to be freed up and grow toward our original design, would Jesus be glad for us? Would it truly be for our best? Would it be surprising if we did not progress well?

Since Jesus perfectly loves us, He desires for our sake that we would succeed in growing well toward our original design. In light of this, He made a pretty blunt statement for our benefit:

> If you love your father or mother more than you love me, you are not worthy of being mine; or if you love your son or daughter more than me, you are not worthy of being mine. If you refuse to take up your cross and follow me, you are not worthy of being mine. If you cling to your life, you will lose it; but if you give up your life for me, you will find it. (Matthew 10:37-39 NLT)

So, in order for us to be able to partake of His forgiveness, we first need to be willing to agree to His conditions that are needed for us to succeed.

Interestingly, this Matthew 10:37-39 passage gives us a wonderful example of how Jesus is infinitely wise and is the best coach. If we did not know that Jesus is perfect in motives and only wants our best, we might incorrectly conclude that He is being selfish in wanting us to not love others more than Him. But, this passage gives us one of the keys to growing toward deeper friendships with Jesus and others. It shows us that we are designed to give our hearts first to Jesus, not to humans. And as our hearts are open and close to Jesus (i.e. a key part of the faucet hookup), the flow of His love will increase through us. This in turn will enable us to have His love for Him, others, and ourselves. This will result in us having much more love for others, including our father and mother, son and daughter, spouse, and many others. Not only this, but we will also avoid a lot of relational hurt that can occur if we give our heart to another person, and then get hurt by that person since the person is not loving all the time like Jesus is.

If you have opened your heart to others and have been really hurt by them, the thought of opening and giving your heart to Jesus may seem scary to you. You may wonder if by doing so, you will get hurt by Jesus or others. Because Jesus perfectly loves you, He will **never** do the relational violation of emotionally "knifing" you. So, you do not have to worry about getting your heart hurt by Jesus. But you might think, "What about other people? If I open my heart to Jesus, will that mean that others will be able to hurt my heart more?" Fortunately, there is an authority that Jesus gives with His love that can help protect our hearts from others, and yet allow them to stay open to Jesus and still have His love for other people. As we grow in our friendship with Jesus and learn from Him, He can teach us how to protect our hearts by not giving our hearts to others and also by not receiving hurtful things from them. Since this is a learning process, some hurtful things may still get through. Fortunately, Jesus is also able to heal the wounds of our hearts if we ask Him to do so.

Even if all of this makes sense to you, you may still be hesitant to make such a large commitment with your life, since you may not know all the details that are involved. So, you might ask me, "Well, you have been growing in your partnership with Jesus for a few decades, what is all involved?" The honest answer I could give you is that growth at times is quite challenging, and yet incredibly worthwhile! Jesus is an expert coach who does not compromise the training requirements needed for us to grow and be freed into our original design. And fortunately, Jesus knows exactly what He is doing and does so only for our very best!

One example of the challenging aspect of growth is found in what Jesus stated about forgiveness. Jesus said that if we do not forgive others, then God will not forgive us. (See Matthew 6:15.) I have at times found it challenging to forgive others who have been mean to me. And yet, I now see that it is a great freedom for me to be able to forgive others even when they do not ask me to forgive them. This way I am not controlled by having grudges toward other people. I also now see that if I hold a grudge toward one person, it will hinder me from loving Jesus and others – since such a grudge puts a kink in the garden hose, which in turn hinders the water of God's love from flowing through me. So, depending on what relational violations others have done to you, this may be a **very** challenging thing for you. Fortunately, if we are willing, Jesus can empower us to be able to do such amazing things as forgiving others.

A second example is one which may not be obvious at first, but is very real none the less. It is the demonic forces that will hate and tempt you all the more because of their hating God's Holy Spirit within you as well as hating you loving and being a good friend to God. Fortunately, Jesus will protect you and limit how much these demons can do to you. The measure of what Jesus allows you to bear will be at times like a refiner's fire for removing dross from a precious metal. But fortunately, Jesus limits the refining and trials to the minimal amount needed for the maximum benefit! Even though I have found this to be very challenging at times, I also smile at the realization that this process is very worthwhile in how Jesus uses it to help me grow in character and to function all the more according to my original design for deeper friendships. And not only does it have benefit for life on earth, but for eternity in heaven as well!

Since you may want to know more about what I'm talking about in terms of these demonic forces, I thought it would be nice and possibly helpful if I gave you a fuller explanation before continuing on...

Many years ago, there were many angels who became arrogant, rejected Jesus, broke their friendship with Jesus, and turned toward all kinds of evil. God eventually gave them the absolutely perfect sentence of justice that their actions deserved, including removing them from heaven. These fallen angels are also known as demons, and because they lost their positions in heaven and because of the evil they have embraced, they are now motivated first and foremost by their totally unjustified, extremely intense hatred toward God. Due to this, demons now have intense hatred at the very core of their being where they not only have extreme hatred for God, but they also have an incredible amount of hatred toward all humans as well!

The demons' hatred of humans is further fueled by their desire to be mean to God, where they indirectly attempt to be mean to God by trying to hinder humans from growing toward friendship with the God who has created them and loves them. Instead of wanting people to function according to the original design to love God, others, and themselves, these demons try to get people to do many relational violations that will result in the people hating God, others, and even themselves.

So if you enter into a close friendship with Jesus, including receiving God's Holy Spirit to dwell within you, then the demons will hate you all the more – both out of their extreme hatred toward the God who now dwells within you, and also because they especially hate anyone actually loving and being a good friend to God. In this, they will be mean and tempt you like they do to all humans – but in an even greater way.

These demons are very smart and often won't use a direct, obvious attack against you that you would easily recognize as working against deeper friendships. Instead, they will subtly tempt you in your thoughts, emotions, feelings, and desires to do things that may seem appealing to you, but the temptation is built by them in such a way that if you are lured away by the temptation, you will first need to do the relational violation of pulling your heart away from God, closing your heart toward God, and even hardening your heart toward God – all of which will kink the garden hose and stop the flow of God's Holy Spirit so that you will not be able to love God, others, and yourself.

The demons will also tempt others to do relational violations against you, and will then tempt you to react in a way that causes you to do relational violations in return. For example, the demons might tempt someone to gloat over you, judge you, reject you, and/or be mean to you in some way. And if instead of turning the other cheek, you follow the temptation to judge, get mad at, and reject that person, it will cause a relational violation kink in the hose that will prevent you from continuing to have God's love for not only that person, but for God, others, and yourself as well.

Like I said earlier, the demons intensely hate all people and tempt all people. So, you will be tempted whether or not you enter into a friendship with Jesus. But, if you do enter into a friendship with Jesus, He will limit how much you are tempted and He will help you to overcome temptations as is stated in the following verse:

> No temptation has overtaken you except what is common to mankind. And God is faithful; he will not let you be tempted beyond what you can bear. But when you are tempted, he will also provide a way out so that you can endure it. (1 Corinthians 10:13)

Fortunately, having God's Holy Spirit on the inside of oneself is fantastic, including that the Holy Spirit is infinitely more powerful than all the demons put together! And learning to rely on God's Holy Spirit is one of the keys to overcoming temptation – where not only will God help us to realize when and how we are being tempted, but He will also show us how to overcome temptation through His power and enabling. This is one of the keys for us growing toward deeper friendships.

With all of these details about demonic forces and temptation explained, I'll now continue…

Now that we looked at some of the challenges and benefits of what is needed on our part, there is still a catch-22 in looking at joining a friendship partnership with Jesus. And that is even if you read many additional details as to what is involved, you still would not fully know what it is like unless you actually partner with Jesus for a while. It would be like if you were single and I was trying to explain to you what married life is like. You have a free choice to say "I do" or not to the marriage relationship. But the catch-22 is that you still will not know all that is required, unless you have experiential firsthand knowledge of being married. After twenty years of marriage, you probably would have a much better idea of what is required to have a growing marriage. But you cannot have twenty years of married experience without saying, "I do," at the start. Also, the unique circumstances of your life are most likely not exactly the same as mine. But, fortunately there are some things that can help you with this decision that have more to do with who Jesus is as your partner than with the particular details of how such a partnership would be for you.

The first thing is the character and desires of God that we looked at in chapter three. I will restate them here:

Some of God's Desires

~ He desires our best (Jeremiah 29:11).

~ He desires a close relationship with us (John 15:15; Matthew 23:37).

~ He desires for us to value ourselves, others, and God (Matthew 22:34-40).

~ He desires that we would know that we are significant, both at the present time and throughout eternity (John 13:1-5; Isaiah 49:15-16; Revelation 2:17; 3:12).

~ He desires that we would be set free into His very best for our lives (John 8:36; 10:10).

Some of God's Characteristics

It is easy to attribute human motives and characteristics to God. But there will always be an "Other-ness" to God—aspects of His character that no human could ever attain. Here is a list of such characteristics:

~ He always wants our best (Romans 8:28).

~ He is always perfect in His motives (Isaiah 55:8-9).

~ He infinitely values us (1 Peter 1:18-19; Romans 5:6-11).

~ He is never partial (Romans 2:11; 1 Peter 1:17).

~ He never commits injustice (2 Chronicles 19:7).

~ He never lies (Numbers 23:19; John 14:6).

~ He always has selfless love toward us (1 John 4:8; Jeremiah 31:3; Psalm 36:5-7).

~ He is infinitely knowledgeable and wise (Romans 11:33-36;

DEEPER FRIENDSHIPS | 185

Isaiah 40:28).

~ He knows us completely (Matthew 10:30; Psalm 139:1-18).

~ He never makes a mistake (2 Samuel 22:31; Deuteronomy 32:4).

~ His character and desires have always been and will always be consistent throughout eternity (Hebrews 13:8).

It is encouraging to know that Jesus is infinitely wise and knows exactly what is needed for us to be freed up and grow into our true design. This is much better than being coached by someone who does not really know what they are doing. It is also nice to know that Jesus is perfect in love and motives toward us. In this, Jesus will never cause a relational violation toward us, but will instead consistently help us each step of the way.

Secondly, if we come into relationship with Jesus, He is the one who provides the water that is needed to water the garden. In other words, Jesus is the one who provides His Holy Spirit that we can receive so that His Holy Spirit within us will then give us what is needed for the fruit of the Holy Spirit to come forth in our lives. It is as if we have a car that does not have an engine, and we try to push that car down the road. The car works much better when it has an engine, is turned on, put in gear, and is driven down the road. Receiving God's Holy Spirit within us is like getting the engine put in the car and having the engine started. Growth is being able to learn both how to put the car in gear and to drive well – which sure beats trying to push the car!

Lastly, I find it helpful to realize that Jesus does not need us in any way. Instead, it is only out of His kindness and perfect love for us that He offers us to join Him in a partnership of friendship. It is first for our sake and then secondly for Him. It is definitely an amazing privilege for us! As Genesis 15:1 says that He truly is our very great reward!

186 | FOUR IN ONE
So, if you would like to join a partnership of friendship with Jesus, including agreeing to the conditions needed to succeed that were outlined in this section, then the following section will give you the actual steps you can take to get repaired and hooked up.

The Actual Steps

Someone might describe the following steps a little differently than I do, and these steps may work a little differently for you than they did for me, but from experience I can assure you that they are steps that actually work.

If you are proceeding with these steps, you have already taken the first step of being willing to agree to God's conditions that were outlined in the last section.

The second step is to open wide your heart to Jesus. So, instead of being at arms length and holding yourself away from Jesus, it is to open up to Him and say to Him something like, "Ok, I open and give my heart to You."

The final step is for you to say something like this out loud to Jesus, "Jesus, I give my life to you for you to coach and grow me toward deeper friendships and all that You have for me. According to what You have done for me on the cross, I ask that You would forgive me for all the relational violations I have done toward You, others, and myself. I also ask You to heal my heart of all the relational violations that others have done to me. And I invite You to come inside of me in a great measure of Your Holy Spirit and have the water of Your Holy Spirit begin to flow through me. And please teach me and help me to grow well all the days of my life in all that You have for me, as You restore me to the original design of who I truly am."

If you have taken these steps, then I congratulate you and welcome you to an incredible journey that will be challenging and yet rewarding. A journey that you will find over time resonates with the very core of your being as being both good and right, and you will know deep down that it is an excellent path for you to be on. You will be especially glad as you see the good fruits and vegetables emerging in the garden of your friendships, which in turn will help you to realize it is truly the best path you could have possibly chosen.

Summary

In this chapter we looked at how the garden hose could be restored to the outdoor faucet, and how this is a simple metaphor that barely describes the beyond-our-comprehension amazing thing that God did for us on the cross to provide the means for us to be healed, forgiven, and restored to a partnership of friendship with Him. God's action was definitely off the charts in terms of His sacrificial love for us! We also looked at what is needed on our part to partake of this wonderful offer. If you have taken these steps now or at some point in the past, I congratulate you and am glad for you, since these steps are needed for each of us to grow toward deeper friendships with Jesus and each other.

Chapter 6 – Conclusion and Next Steps

As a woman reflected upon her life, she realized she had spent many years in what seemed like an extremely large maze. As much as she had tried to diligently find her way out, she only found an endless labyrinth of passageways and dead ends. Each time she reached a dead end, she would feel a little more discouraged that she was still stuck in the maze. But her strong desire to eventually find a way out continued to motivate her to turn around and continue her diligent search. After many years of searching and finding only dead ends, she began to wonder if she would ever find her way out. But she knew such thoughts would only slow her down in her quest. So she determined that no matter how many discouraging thoughts would cross her mind, she would still try to continue onward.

One day as the woman was trying once again to find her way out, she walked down a sequence of hallways, and instead of hitting the usual dead end, she found a door. She became very excited, since it was the first door she had ever seen in the maze. Next to the door were many keys hung upon the wall. As she looked at the keys for a while, she took a rough estimate and guessed there were at least three or four thousand keys. Even though there were so many keys, she became very excited at the thought that hopefully one of them would enable her to get out of the maze! So, she quickly began to take each key, place it in the door lock, turn it as far as it would go, and then push on the door to see if it would open. But each time, the door would not budge.

After hundreds and hundreds of keys, the woman began to get quite discouraged. She began to wonder if any of the keys would even work, and even if one did work, would it really be a way out or only lead to another sequence of passageways and dead ends? As she thought about turning around and looking for another way out of the maze, she realized that if she did so, she might never find her way back to this door which could possibly be her only way out. So she decided that no matter how long it might take, she would try every one of the keys.

After many hours and many more keys, the woman found a key that turned further in the lock than the others had. As she continued to turn the key she heard a click. She then pushed on the door, and it began to open! Her excitement level skyrocketed! As she opened the door she saw sunshine for the first time and before her was a beautiful meadow!

The woman was so thankful she had found the key that had worked, that she took the key out of the door lock and took it with her as she walked out into the sunlit meadow. With the light being better outside than in the maze, she could now see that there were letters engraved on the key. As her eyes adjusted to the light, she looked closer at the letters and saw that it said, "Friendship with Jesus is the key to life."

Years later, as the woman reflected back on these events that had occurred in her life, she realized that friendship with Jesus had indeed unlocked what she had always been looking for in that it had opened the way toward wonderful friendships with Jesus and others. A big smile broke across her face as she became so very thankful that she not only finally knew why she existed, but that she had found the greatest treasure of knowing Jesus as her best friend!

***** **End of Story** *****

Like the woman in this story, I too am very thankful and feel very fortunate to have found that the key to life is friendship with Jesus. I hope this conclusion is easily seen from what I shared in the prior chapters. I also hope this book has been an inspiration for you to grow in your friendship with Jesus and others as well.

If you asked me to recommend other things that would be helpful to you in growing toward deeper friendships, I would give you the following three suggestions.

The first thing I would suggest is a prayer, in which you would ask Jesus to grow you over time to become a wonderful friend of His. This suggestion is based on the realization that only Jesus can truly grow us toward deeper friendships with Him and others, and therefore it is helpful for us to look to Him to do so.

My second suggestion is that you would get a copy of *At His Feet* (which you can purchase at **www.OrderAtHisFeet.com**). *At His Feet* is a book I wrote especially for a person new to their relationship with God, but it has also proved to be helpful to those who have been in relationship with Jesus for longer periods of time. The reason I suggest *At His Feet* is because it has many practical suggestions for how to grow in one's friendship with Jesus. And growing in our friendship with Jesus is the biggest key to our growing in our friendships with each other. *At His Feet* also has an appendix that gives some practical ways to read the Bible, since the Bible is a fantastic resource that Jesus can use to help us to grow in deeper friendships.

My third suggestion is for the future. I hope someday to write additional books that are very practical and helpful for one's life with Jesus. So, if and when these books become available, I hope they turn out to be quite valuable both to you and to others as well.

Thank you for allowing me to share my heart with you through this book. I hope the things I shared have already been helpful to you, and in the future will continue to be helpful to you in your journey toward deeper friendships.

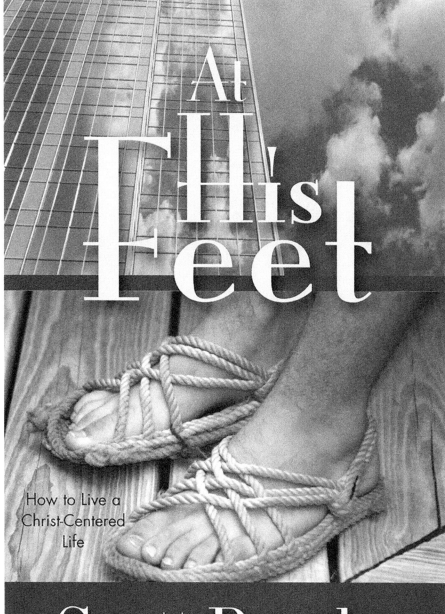

At His Feet

How to Live a
Christ-Centered
Life

Scott Brooks

At His Feet

By Scott Brooks

Gazelle

ISBN 1-58169-172-6
For Worldwide Distribution
Printed in the U.S.A.

Gazelle Press
P.O. Box 191540 • Mobile, AL 36619
800-367-8203

Author's Note

The rights to **At His Feet** were purchased by Scott Brooks from Gazelle Press in 2015.

Table of Contents for Book 4 – *At His Feet*

Dedication

I dedicate this book to the One to whom I owe my very existence...
the One at whose feet I love to sit.

Introduction

The Bible speaks of a woman named Martha who invited Jesus into
her home. While Martha was busy with preparations for the meal, her
sister, Mary, sat at Jesus' feet, spending time with Him and learning
from Him. As Martha became more and more stressed and uptight
because of the cooking and housework, she became upset that Mary
wasn't helping with the preparations. Finally, Martha interrupted her
sister's time with the Lord. Martha told Jesus that she didn't think
it was fair that she was doing all of the work, and then she asked
Jesus to tell Mary to help her. Jesus kindly responded by telling her
that while she was worried and upset about many things, Mary had
discovered what was better and that her time with Him would not be
taken from her. (See Luke 10:38-42.)

I love this passage of the Bible. When I picture Mary sitting at the feet
of Jesus, the Lord of the universe, learning from Him and growing
in her friendship with Him, it stirs something warm in my heart, and
I desire to live my life from that same place—at the feet of my Lord.
I think, *Wow, what a privilege to be with Jesus, to learn from Him,
and to grow in friendship with Him! He is the best Friend I could
ever have—the One who is perfect in character and cares for me
completely. I can think of no higher privilege than to live life from this
place—at Jesus' feet!*

During the times I've lived at Jesus' feet, I've seen God bring forth
good things through His Holy Spirit within me, including the fruit of the
Spirit: "love, joy, peace, patience, kindness, goodness, faithfulness,
gentleness and self-control" (Galatians 5:22-23). In turn, these "good
things" have positively affected my relationship with God and my
relationships with my family, friends, and other people.

Contained within the pages of this book are practical ideas and
suggestions that can help both you and me to grow in living at Jesus'
feet. I am incomplete in my understanding of all that is needed to do
this well, but in this book I share those things that I have found to be

helpful in my life. I have a strong desire to keep these things in focus, for I know if I lose sight of them, then I will miss what is most important in life—those things that are God's best for me.

In one of my past summer jobs, I had a boss whom I really appreciated. My boss did not make any assumptions as to what I knew or didn't know. Instead, he shared with me all the details that I might need to do my job well. Some of these things I already knew, but there were some things of which I wasn't aware. I was very thankful that he shared every detail with me so that I could see what I was missing and in what areas I needed to grow.

In a similar way, I will include in this book many details about what is needed to live our lives well at Jesus' feet. If you have already been in relationship with God for a long time, my desire is that God would bring these details to life inside of you and refresh your perspective on those things that are critical to your life with Him. On the other hand, if you are brand new in your relationship with God, my desire is that God would bring these details to life in your heart and cause them to be of great value to you throughout your life with Him. If you have never read the Bible, I hope the many Scripture passages included in this book will provide you with an exciting introduction to the riches of God's Word. The Bible is a powerful tool that God can use in all of our hearts and lives.

The content in this book is very valuable to me, and I always want to keep it as the focus of my life. One of the reasons I am writing this book is so that I can periodically read it every year or two in order to focus and refocus upon these important things. I'm also writing this book for you, and I welcome you to join me in keeping these important things in view. My desire is that both you and I would grow and blossom into what is God's best for us, as we live our lives at this very privileged place—at His feet.

Every time I read this book, I plan to ask God to soften my heart and cause things to stand out to me. This way, each time I read it,

God will illuminate the things that are most relevant to my life at that time. I welcome you to join me in asking God for the same thing—a softened heart and His illumination of the things most pertinent to your life. Hopefully you will not just read what I have written, but you will also hear what God wants to speak to you through this book. I truly hope that you find this book to be of great value in your life, that you are encouraged at how God uses it in your life, and that it will be an encouragement for you to continue to live your life well **at Jesus' feet**.

—Scott Brooks, 2005

Chapter 1 – Having Soft and Teachable Hearts

There was once a man who had such a bad heart condition that it eventually killed him. But his condition wasn't an issue of the hardening of his arteries or any other disease in his heart—it was his spiritual heart that had hardened. Because of this condition, the man made all sorts of poor decisions in his life. Unfortunately, this man was a man of influence, and due to his poor decisions, terrible destruction came to the country he ruled, including the deaths of many people and the loss of his own life, as well.

If you have not guessed it already, I'm writing about Pharaoh, the ruler of Egypt at the time of Moses, the man who hardened his heart against God over and over again.

In stark contrast to Pharaoh's attitude toward God, we have the picture of Mary, the sister of Martha, humbly sitting at Jesus' feet. Mary had a soft, teachable heart, as opposed to Pharaoh's arrogant one.

In this chapter, we'll take a look at this very important issue of our spiritual heart condition. We'll examine our spiritual hearts, as well as explore some of the keys to having "good" hearts before God, so that, like Mary, we can also blossom at the feet of Jesus.

What Do Our Hearts Look Like?

Jesus once told a parable that explains what our spiritual hearts are like. In the story, a farmer sowed seed, which fell on various types of ground: Some fell on the footpath, some fell on shallow soil, some on thorny ground, and still others in fertile soil. The seed only grew well in the fertile soil, where it produced a bountiful harvest. When His disciples asked Him the following question, Jesus' answer reveals much about the human heart.

His disciples came and asked him, "Why do you always tell

stories when you talk to the people?" Then he explained to them, "You have been permitted to understand the secrets of the Kingdom of Heaven, but others have not. To those who are open to my teaching, more understanding will be given, and they will have an abundance of knowledge. But to those who are not listening, even what they have will be taken away from them. That is why I tell these stories, because people see what I do, but they don't really see. They hear what I say, but they don't really hear, and they don't understand. This fulfills the prophecy of Isaiah, which says:

'You will hear my words, but you will not understand; you will see what I do, but you will not perceive its meaning. For the hearts of these people are hardened, and their ears cannot hear, and they have closed their eyes—so their eyes cannot see, and their ears cannot hear, and their hearts cannot understand, and they cannot turn to me and let me heal them.'

But blessed are your eyes, because they see; and your ears, because they hear. I assure you, many prophets and godly people have longed to see and hear what you have seen and heard, but they could not (Matthew 13:10-17).

Jesus then went on to explain the meaning of the parable to His disciples. Jesus is the farmer, and the seed is the word He sows. The various types of ground represented the various types of people's hearts that hear His word. Different hearts receive His word in different ways, and there are many things that can hinder us from having good "heart soil" before God. We face many temptations that can hinder us from growing, just as the seeds faced adverse conditions when they fell on the thorny ground. If our hearts become hard like the footpath soil, they will be poor receptors of His word, and we won't learn well at Jesus' feet. But if we have responsive hearts before God and receive His word as the fertile soil received the seed, we will grow and be fruitful in those things that are God's best for us.

There is another Bible passage that provides us with a helpful key as to how we can have good heart soil.

> Great crowds were following Jesus. He turned around and said to them, "If you want to be my follower you must love me more than your own father and mother, wife and children, brothers and sisters—yes, more than your own life. Otherwise, you cannot be my disciple. And you cannot be my disciple if you do not carry your own cross and follow me. But don't begin until you count the cost. For who would begin construction of a building without first getting estimates and then checking to see if there is enough money to pay the bills? Otherwise, you might complete only the foundation before running out of funds. And then how everyone would laugh at you! They would say, "There's the person who started that building and ran out of money before it was finished!"

> Or what king would ever dream of going to war without first sitting down with his counselors and discussing whether his army of ten thousand is strong enough to defeat the twenty thousand soldiers who are marching against him? If he is not able, then while the enemy is still far away, he will send a delegation to discuss terms of peace. So no one can become my disciple without giving up everything for me. Salt is good for seasoning. But if it loses its flavor, how do you make it salty again? Flavorless salt is good neither for the soil nor for fertilizer. It is thrown away. Anyone who is willing to hear should listen and understand! (Luke 14:25-35)

At times I have found this passage of Scripture to be very challenging. People who are reading this passage for the first time might even wonder if Jesus were setting an unrealistically high standard, or at least they might think that these instructions would infringe too much on their lives. But the more I learn, the more I realize that this is actually a wonderful passage, one that provides tremendous freedom for all of us. It contains an important key to creating fertile soil within our hearts. You may wonder how I would reach such a conclusion; part of the answer comes out of this simple question: "Who is smarter, God or me?" Obviously, the answer is that God (and likewise, Jesus) is much smarter than I am, much more than I can even begin to fathom. So, if Jesus has made each of the following statements, did He really know what He was saying? Of course, He did!

> If you want to be My follower, you must love Me more than you love your own father or mother, wife or children, brothers or sisters—yes, even more than your own life. Otherwise, you cannot be My disciple.

> And you cannot be My disciple if you do not carry your own cross and follow me.

> No one can become My disciple without giving up everything for Me.

I find that if I first commit myself to God and trust in His infinite wisdom, over time as I begin to see Him working in my life, I will eventually learn what He already knew all along. In the Parable of the Sower, the seeds had difficulty growing in different soil conditions. Fortunately, God already knows the very best ways to keep our hearts fertile, as good soil, which produces a harvest of fruit.

Consider this analogy: Imagine that God is an expert instructor in music, particularly in teaching the guitar. I decide that I want to learn to play the guitar, but I also decide that I want to do it my own way and not pay attention to His instructions. Deep down I really feel that His instruction is not all that important. With this mindset, should I be surprised at how slowly I progress? But if I have the humility to realize that He is the Master Instructor, and if I am able to wholeheartedly give myself to Him and accept His teaching, then He truly can make me into an accomplished guitarist.

In my own life, there have been numerous occasions in which I hit a spiritual "wall." When I finally looked to God, He helped me realize that I didn't know as much as I thought I did, and He had much better ways for me to get to excellent places. A great example of this occurred when I was still an atheist, but near the point of entering into a relationship with God. I had tried numerous philosophies and other attempts at happiness, but no matter how hard I tried, my desires would still conflict with each other. I couldn't get my desires to mesh with each other toward a common goal. I was tired of trying to find happiness over and over again, and still winding up empty. When I finally came to the decision to enter into a relationship with God, I concluded that I had diligently tried everything else unsuccessfully. I decided that I had nothing else to lose—I would give my life to God to see what He could do with it. It was then that I started to learn that He is more than capable of bringing good things into my life.

My life is a lot like strands of rope that get knotted into a ball, and the more I work at the knots the worse they get. Fortunately I can give the knotted ball to Jesus, and I'm glad that He is willing to untangle the knots and free my life for His purposes. As I continue to daily commit my life to God, I see Him changing my heart into good soil and causing me to grow in fruitful ways as He frees me from snares, temptations, and lures. He also waters me with His love, and I see Him causing me to grow in understanding and character. It is wonderful to see this affect my entire life, including my relationships with my wife and children. This all confirms His plan to me and helps me to know, deep down, that He indeed does know what He is doing, and His path is truly the best path for me to take—even if it is challenging at times.

As I said earlier, it sometimes takes time to see what God is doing in our lives. If our focus is, "I've given my life to God; now what am I going to get out of the deal?" and we are only concerned with short-term gain (although it may not truly be gain), then it would be all too easy to find ourselves among the thorns, or worse.

But like young plants in such soil, their roots don't go very deep. At first they get along fine, but they wilt as soon as they have problems or are persecuted because they believe the word. The thorny ground represents those who hear and accept the Good News, but all too quickly the message is crowded out by the cares of this life and the lure of wealth, so no crop is produced (Matthew 13:21-22).

Jesus has said that we cannot be His disciples unless we carry our crosses and follow Him. He has also said that no one can be His disciple unless they give up everything for Him. Fortunately, these statements can bring great freedom for us, for as we give our lives fully to Him, He can then bring us to good places in the long run. As Jesus said in John 8:36, "If the Son [Jesus] sets you free, you will indeed be free."

The following story from the Bible gives us a great example of this process. It shows us if we will pick up our crosses and tag along with God in His best for us, God knows exactly what He is doing and will even surprise us at times at what He can wonderfully bring about in our lives.

God had promised Abraham that he and his wife, Sarah, would bear a child even though they were both very old, and Sarah was well past her childbearing years. God also promised that Abraham would have many blessed offspring through this child. Things worked out just as God had promised: Sarah miraculously became pregnant and gave birth to a son, whom they named Isaac. Abraham knew that Isaac was the key to God's promise that he would be the father of many nations.

Abraham was given a test by the Lord, a test that at first seemed to be too difficult to imagine: God asked him to sacrifice his beloved son Isaac, the son of God's promise. Although Abraham struggled with this test, he eventually found the courage to follow through with what God challenged him to do. Because of Abraham's obedience, the Lord provided a ram to take Isaac's place on the altar of sacrifice, and Abraham received this word of promise:

> This is what the Lord says: Because you have obeyed me and
> have not withheld even your beloved son, I swear by my own
> self that I will bless you richly. I will multiply your descendants
> into countless millions, like the stars of the sky and the sand
> on the seashore. They will conquer their enemies, and through
> your descendants, all the nations of the earth will be blessed—
> all because you have obeyed me (Genesis 22:16-18).

Abraham was challenged by what God asked him to do, just as we
are challenged when Jesus asks us to pick up our crosses and follow
Him every day. But Abraham found the courage to follow through with
what God challenged him to do, and because of this, he was given a
beautiful freedom.

Although it is not explicitly stated in the text, in his heart, it is likely that
Abraham took hold of Isaac in unhealthy ways. This, in turn, hindered
Abraham from being good soil before God and becoming all that God
knew he could become. God's challenge to Abraham helped him to
have the freedom of which Jesus would speak centuries later:

> Jesus said, "If you want to be my follower you must love me
> more than your own father and mother, wife and children,
> brothers and sisters—yes, more than your own life. Otherwise,
> you cannot be my disciple" (Luke 14:26).

By being obedient to God's command to sacrifice his son, Abraham
essentially gave Isaac back over to God and was freed in his heart
of an unhealthy bond. Isaac was then God's first, not Abraham's first,
and Abraham was freed to be an excellent father, a steward of his
son through God's help. Abraham's heart was freed to first have a
primary relationship with God, which would then affect all of his other
relationships. As long as Isaac held the primary place in his heart, it
was hindering this freedom. It wasn't that God wanted to take Isaac
from Abraham, but he wanted to free Abraham from trying to carry
what is best carried by God.

206 | FOUR IN ONE

Dealing with Fears

It can be a scary thing to come before God and wholeheartedly put the entirety of our lives on His altar, including all of our relationships, our desires, our goals, and even our personalities. And yet, if we look at many examples in the Bible, we find that when people go through this process, God frees them to grow in love, joy, peace, and all of the other good things He has for them. If we are afraid, and if we hold back areas of our lives from God, it might seem like a good idea in the short run, but it will ultimately hinder the tremendous growth process that God wants to bring about in our lives.

As a child, if I had a splinter in my hand, I would go to my mom or dad for help. It was a bit frightening to put my hand in theirs and allow them to work with the tweezers to remove the splinter. But the only way that the splinter could be removed and that my hand could heal to fully function as it was intended to, would be for me to have enough courage to hold my hand steadily in theirs. My parents knew that I might experience some pain in the process, but they were willing to allow this minor pain and discomfort to take place because they knew it was what I needed. In a similar way, God isn't interested in ruining our fun or taking things that we like away from us. Instead, He knows the entire process of our lives, and He knows exactly what is needed to get us to where we can function fully as we were designed to function, even if it requires some suffering on our part or some changes in our lives.

The process of the altar brings us to the place in which we give our entire lives to God, allowing Him to sacrifice those things that hinder us from growing in Him. In turn, He enhances those aspects of our character that are already good. So if we give the entirety of our lives to Him—including what we do with our time, what we do with our energy, our decisions as to where we will go or what we will do—then God can direct us into good things in our lives. But the most important requirement is our willingness to place ourselves entirely in God's hands.

Many of us still experience trepidation when it comes to surrendering all of our lives to God. Is there anything else that can help us deal with our fears, so that we can fully place ourselves in God's hands? In my own life, I have found that an understanding of God's desires and characteristics can help us with our fears of surrender.

Some of God's Desires

~ He desires our best (Jeremiah 29:11).

~ He desires a close relationship with us (John 15:15; Matthew 23:37).

~ He desires for us to value ourselves, others, and God (Matthew 22:34-40).

~ He desires that we would know that we are significant, both at the present time and throughout eternity (John 13:1-5; Isaiah 49:15-16; Revelation 2:17; 3:12).

~ He desires that we would be set free into His very best for our lives (John 8:36; 10:10).

Some of God's Characteristics

It is easy to attribute human motives and characteristics to God. But there will always be an "Other-ness" to God— aspects of His character that no human could ever attain. Here is a list of such characteristics:

~ He always wants our best (Romans 8:28).

~ He is always perfect in His motives (Isaiah 55:8-9).

~ He infinitely values us (1 Peter 1:18-19; Romans 5:6-11).

~ He is never partial (Romans 2:11; 1 Peter 1:17).

~ He never commits injustice (2 Chronicles 19:7).

~ He never lies (Numbers 23:19; John 14:6).

~ He always has selfless love toward us (1 John 4:8; Jeremiah 31:3; Psalm 36:5-7).

~ He is infinitely knowledgeable and wise (Romans 11:33-36; Isaiah 40:28).

~ He knows us completely (Matthew 10:30; Psalm 139:1-18).

~ He never makes a mistake (2 Samuel 22:31; Deuteronomy 32:4).

~ His character and desires have always been and will always be consistent throughout eternity (Hebrews 13:8).

These lists have been derived from many Bible verses. I have also found them to be consistent with my own personal experience with God and what I have experienced of reality.

Side Note: If you would like to learn more about these desires and characteristics of God, the verses in the parentheses should give you a good place to start.

If we take time to ponder each of God's desires and characteristics, we will begin to realize how very fortunate we are to have such a wonderful Being to whom we can entrust our lives. It's amazing to realize that He loves and values us intimately, that He knows us completely, that He always wants our best, and that He never makes a mistake. It's also comforting to know that because God wants our best, He will not take us through anything or have us change in any way that would not be good for us. God will never use acceptance or rejection to try to control us. He always loves us, even when we do wrong, and in this love, He helps us to turn from our sins, receive forgiveness through His redeeming work on the cross, and then move on toward what is best for our lives.

There is value in knowing God's desires and character. Trusting in His character is a lot like trusting in an excellent surgeon. If I needed a difficult surgery, I would most likely ask around to find a specialist in that field who had a great reputation. If many people spoke highly of a particular surgeon and attested to the excellent results they had experienced, my confidence in that surgeon would naturally grow, and I would feel more comfortable entrusting my case to him. In a similar way, God's working in the lives of others demonstrates His perfect character. When I read the Bible and see how God has worked in other people's lives, I am encouraged to trust my own life to Him even more. And when other people share with me what God has done in their lives, it inspires me to give my life fully to Him for Him to work out what is best for me.

Taking small steps to trust in God—and in His desires and character—leads to the ability to then take larger steps. If there were a rickety bridge that spanned a raging river, we might "trust" in that bridge all we wanted, but we might still find that if we step out on it, we could fall through and be swept away. But if there were a well-built, solid bridge over that same raging river, then we might still be fearful, but as we step onto the bridge, we find that it truly holds our weight. The more steps we take, the more we realize the solidness of the bridge and our overall confidence increases. In this process, our first steps might be easier if we knew the bridge's architect and his/her excellent reputation in building only solid, high-tolerance bridges.

At one point in his life, Jacob stepped out onto the bridge of trust in God, but only after he had first struck a deal with the Lord:

> Then Jacob made this vow: **"If** God will be with me and protect me on this journey and give me food and clothing, and if he

will bring me back safely to my father, **then I will make the LORD my God"** (Genesis 28:20-21, emphasis mine).

I think it is interesting that God didn't say, "Hey, Jacob, I said to pick up your cross and follow Me fully! Why are you challenging what I said?" Instead, God honored Jacob's request. The text seems to imply that Jacob truly wanted to follow God's best for him, but at the same time, he knew there were things that frightened him. So rather than going forward and becoming more fearful about these things, he instead decided to make a deal with God. Jacob essentially told God that if He would help him with his fears, then he would gladly follow God. God agreed to this deal; not only did He help Jacob to overcome his fears, but He also helped Jacob to pick up his cross and follow after Him. What about us? Would making a deal with God help us with any fear we might have of taking up our own crosses and following the Lord?

There are many other Bible verses that show how God can help us with our fears as we share our concerns with Him.

> Give all your worries and cares to God, for he cares about what happens to you (1 Peter 5:7).

> Don't worry about anything; instead, pray about everything. Tell God what you need, and thank him for all he has done. If you do this, you will experience God's peace, which is far more wonderful than the human mind can understand. His peace will guard your hearts and minds as you live in Christ Jesus (Philippians 4:6-7).

Relationship Is the Key

As we come to the altar and pick up our cross, it can seem very challenging at times. We really need God's enabling and help throughout the whole process. Instead of our accomplishing God's best for us, we actually need God to accomplish it through us. If we think we can do it on our own, we will eventually learn the hard reality that we can't—and that is a difficult lesson to learn. God does not want us to run ahead and do things on our own, but instead walk beside Him, building our relationship and friendship with Him in the process. It's a positive relationship growth cycle: As we live our lives with God, in a growing friendship with Him, we'll be able to receive God's love and draw upon His enabling and provision in an even greater way. God will then use this to deepen and develop our relationship with Him!

Two Sides of the Same Coin

There is a question that is commonly asked by people who are new in their relationship with God:

> "I committed my life to God and received His finished work on the cross so that I could be forgiven and enter into a relationship with Him. And I thought it was only through this completed work of Jesus on the cross that I am in relationship with God and will go to heaven someday. Yet in this chapter, you seem to imply that we can't be in relationship with God (and eventually enter heaven) unless we pick up our cross and follow Jesus daily. Are these contradictory concepts, or do they work together somehow?"

What we are actually looking at are two sides of the same coin. On one side of the coin, we are not worthy to be God's disciples, and we will not make it to heaven unless, by His grace and enabling, we:

~ Daily pick up our cross and follow Him (Luke 14:27).

~ Wholeheartedly follow God's best for us (Romans 6:17).

~ Refuse to forsake our first love of God (Revelation 2:4-7).

~ Overcome any temptations that try to keep us from God's

best for us (Revelation 3:4-6).

~ Prove ourselves faithful to God (1 Corinthians 4:2).

Side Note: I have listed the Scripture references in the parentheses above in case you were interested in reading in the Bible where these concepts are explicitly discussed.

On the other side of the coin is Jesus' payment for us on the cross and His conquest of death by His resurrection. Only because of Jesus' payment for our sins are we made acceptable before God. We do not deserve this at all, but because we have received God's amazing gift of love, we are adopted into God's family and become heirs of His promises. Without Jesus' work on our behalf, none of us would ever be good enough to enter into a relationship with God or to go to heaven. Also on this side of the coin are God's promises for our own lives. As we daily commit our lives to Him and wholeheartedly follow Him in His best for us, He is faithful to bring about good things in our lives and eventually bring us to heaven.

Peter wrote about both sides of the coin in the following passage:

> As we know Jesus better, his divine power gives us everything we need for living a godly life. He has called us to receive his own glory and goodness! And by that same mighty power, he has given us all of his rich and wonderful promises. He has promised that you will escape the decadence all around you caused by evil desires and that you will share in his divine nature. So make every effort to apply the benefits of these promises to your life. Then your faith will produce a life of moral excellence. A life of moral excellence leads to knowing God better.
>
> Knowing God leads to self-control. Self-control leads to patient endurance, and patient endurance leads to godliness. Godliness leads to love for other Christians, and finally you will

grow to have genuine love for everyone. The more you grow like this, the more you will become productive and useful in your knowledge of our Lord Jesus Christ. But those who fail to develop these virtues are blind or, at least, very shortsighted. They have already forgotten that God has cleansed them from their old life of sin. So, dear brothers and sisters, work hard to prove that you really are among those God has called and chosen. Doing this, you will never stumble or fall away. And God will open wide the gates of heaven for you to enter into the eternal Kingdom of our Lord and Savior Jesus Christ (2 Peter 1:3-11).

Summary

In this chapter we have explored some of the keys needed for us to have soft, teachable hearts that learn from Jesus as Mary did. The rest of this book builds upon these keys. One key is that we wholeheartedly pick up our cross and follow Jesus. Another key is that we lay down our lives on God's altar. But the greatest key is that we focus on our relationship with God and look to Him to accomplish all of this through us, as He draws us near to Him in our hearts. This might seem frightening at first, but understanding God's good desires and His characteristics that work for our freedom and for our very best, is key to our being able to trust Him in this excellent process.

I'd like to end this chapter with two passages from Scripture that are meaningful to me. These passages tie many of this chapter's concepts together. As you read, please notice the words that I have bolded for further emphasis and then bring these verses before God and ask Him to show you the meaning He has for them in your life.

> Jesus said, "If you try to keep your life for yourself, you will lose it. But if you give up your life for me, **you will find true life**" (Matthew 16:25, emphasis mine).

> Jesus said, "I am the true vine, and my Father is the gardener.

He cuts off every branch that doesn't produce fruit, and he prunes the branches that do bear fruit **so they will produce even more**. You have already been pruned for greater fruitfulness by the message I have given you. Remain in me, and I will remain in you. For a branch cannot produce fruit if it is severed from the vine, and you cannot be fruitful apart from me. Yes, I am the vine; you are the branches. **Those who remain in me, and I in them, will produce much fruit. For apart from me you can do nothing.** Anyone who parts from me is thrown away like a useless branch and withers. Such branches are gathered into a pile to be burned. **But if you stay joined to me and my words remain in you,** you may ask any request you like, and it will be granted!

My true disciples produce much fruit. This brings great glory to my Father. I have loved you even as the Father has loved me. **Remain in my love.** When you obey me, you remain in my love, just as I obey my Father and remain in his love. I have told you this so that you will be filled with my joy. Yes, your joy will overflow! I command you to love each other in the same way that I love you.

And here is how to measure it—the greatest love is shown when people lay down their lives for their friends. You are my friends if you obey me. I no longer call you servants, because a master doesn't confide in his servants. Now **you are my friends,** since I have told you everything the Father told me. You didn't choose me. I chose you. I appointed you to go and **produce fruit that will last,** so that the Father will give you whatever you ask for, using my name. I command you to love each other" (John 15:1-17, emphasis mine).

Chapter 2 – The Value and Privilege of Learning From God

Can you imagine what it was like for Mary to sit at the feet of Jesus? Can you imagine what it was like to be able to directly gaze into Jesus' eyes of love, to listen to the love in His voice, to feel so highly valued and cared for by Him who is the God of the universe?

If I had been there at that time, I would have loved to have gone over and sat next to Mary. It would have been such a privilege just to be in Jesus' presence, let alone be able to learn from Him. And if at some point Jesus decided to give out hugs, I would have jumped up to join the line! I also would have enjoyed watching each person smile as Jesus' love abundantly flowed out to them like a river of water.

But here we are in the present day, long after Jesus was resurrected, and He is no longer physically with us like He was with Mary. So, how can we learn from Jesus as Mary did?

In the last chapter, we partially answered that question by discussing a number of prerequisites that are needed if we are to learn from God, such as having a soft and teachable heart, laying down our lives on His altar, realizing that His wisdom is greater than our own, and paying attention to Him as our expert instructor.

In the next chapter we'll answer that question more fully, but for now let's first consider why it is of such value and privilege for us to learn from God.

The Value of Learning from God

It is definitely important for each of us to learn from God. For one reason, it brings great freedom to our lives. It is a lot like learning to read: If we don't know how to read, we will be greatly hindered in life. The list of benefits that literacy brings is practically endless: being able to do your job, learning well in school, reading street signs, even following instructions for putting something together! Without the ability to read, we would need to rely on someone else to read for us in many situations. But if we learn to read for ourselves, we are so much farther along than even if someone were always around to help us. In a similar way, if each of us learns from God, we will bear fruit as the individuals He has designed us to be.

Learning from God ourselves is the key to an important issue I like to call ownership. By "ownership," I mean that it is good for each of us to take personal responsibility to learn from God ourselves. We can certainly benefit from what others have learned from God and are willing to share with us (in much the same way as we benefit from someone else reading for us), but if we only listen to others and do not learn from God ourselves, then we will be greatly disadvantaged and hindered in our growth.

Taking ownership and learning from God ourselves is a lot like driving to a new destination in a car. If we are the one driving, we usually have a much better chance remembering the route than if we are a passenger. It is also like participating in a sporting event or a concert. We can know a lot about a certain sports team or about those playing the instruments at a concert, but we experience a much higher level of ownership if we ourselves are the one playing. It can also be compared to taking a class. It is one thing to memorize the material and to parrot the answers back at test time. But we experience a much higher level of ownership if we have a working knowledge of the material and are able to answer intelligently out of our experience. Taking ownership and learning from God directly is of critical importance to our growing more fruitful in His very best for us. We can see this demonstrated in the following parable:

> Jesus said, "The Kingdom of Heaven can be illustrated by the story of ten bridesmaids who took their lamps and went to meet the bridegroom. Five of them were foolish, and five were wise. The five who were foolish took no oil for their lamps, but the other five were wise enough to take along extra oil. When the bridegroom was delayed, they all lay down and slept. At

midnight they were roused by the shout, 'Look, the bridegroom is coming! Come out and welcome him!'

"All the bridesmaids got up and prepared their lamps. Then the five foolish ones asked the others, 'Please give us some of your oil because our lamps are going out.' But the others replied, 'We don't have enough for all of us. Go to a shop and buy some for yourselves.'

"But while they were gone to buy oil, the bridegroom came, and those who were ready went in with him to the marriage feast, and the door was locked. Later, when the other five bridesmaids returned, they stood outside, calling, 'Sir, open the door for us!' But he called back, 'I don't know you!'

"So stay awake and be prepared, because you do not know the day or hour of my return" (Matthew 25:1-13).

Imagine taking a class that has only one test at the end of the course. How would you feel if you studied very diligently for the test, but as you took it, you realized that you had studied the wrong material? In the parable of the bridesmaids, the foolish bridesmaids were unprepared for the "test." They didn't realize it at first, but when the bridegroom said, "I don't know you," they realized they had failed, and it was too late for them to enter the wedding feast. In contrast, things went very well for the wise bridesmaids. They were prepared, and they were welcomed by the bridegroom.

It is interesting to note that the foolish bridesmaids didn't understand the importance of getting to know God in relationship and were told, "I never knew you." In contrast, it is likely that the wise bridesmaids did well because they wanted to learn from God themselves and were eager to be in a relationship with Him.

The following parable of the three servants also demonstrates the importance of learning from God ourselves.

Jesus said, "Again, the Kingdom of Heaven can be illustrated by the story of a man going on a trip. He called together his servants and gave them money to invest for him while he was gone. He gave five bags of gold to one, two bags of gold to another, and one bag of gold to the last-dividing it in proportion to their abilities—and then left on his trip. The servant who received the five bags of gold began immediately to invest the money and soon doubled it. The servant with two bags of gold also went right to work and doubled the money. But the servant who received the one bag of gold dug a hole in the ground and hid the master's money for safekeeping.

"After a long time their master returned from his trip and called them to give an account of how they had used his money. The servant to whom he had entrusted the five bags of gold said, 'Sir, you gave me five bags of gold to invest, and I have doubled the amount.' The master was full of praise. 'Well done, my good and faithful servant. You have been faithful in handling this small amount, so now I will give you many more responsibilities. Let's celebrate together!'

"Next came the servant who had received the two bags of gold, with the report, 'Sir, you gave me two bags of gold to invest, and I have doubled the amount.' The master said, 'Well done, my good and faithful servant. You have been faithful in handling this small amount, so now I will give you many more responsibilities. Let's celebrate together!'

"Then the servant with the one bag of gold came and said, 'Sir, I know you are a hard man, harvesting crops you didn't plant and gathering crops you didn't cultivate. I was afraid I would lose your money, so I hid it in the earth and here it is.'

"But the master replied, 'You wicked and lazy servant! You think I'm a hard man, do you, harvesting crops I didn't plant and gathering crops I didn't cultivate? Well, you should at least have put my money into the bank so I could have some interest. Take the money from this servant and give it to the one with the ten bags of gold. To those who use well what they are given, even more will be given, and they will have an abundance. But from those who are unfaithful, even what little they have will be taken away. Now throw this useless servant into outer darkness, where there will be weeping and gnashing of teeth' (Matthew 25:14-30).

The servant who hid his money did not have a good understanding of God's character and activity in the world. Instead he thought that God was "a hard man, harvesting crops He didn't plant and gathering crops He didn't cultivate." By hiding his money, he refused to take responsibility for the things that God asked him to do. I don't know what he did after he hid the money, but it obviously wasn't what God wanted him to do, and so, overall, he completely missed out on God's best for his life. The other servants had a good understanding of God and ultimately were fruitful in the things God asked them to do. In turn they became pleasing to God. If we hope to be like these faithful servants, we truly need God as our instructor. The following verses describe God's teaching in terms of the renewing of our minds.

> Therefore, I urge you, brothers, in view of God's mercy, to offer your bodies as living sacrifices, holy and pleasing to God— this is your spiritual act of worship. **Do not conform any longer to the pattern of this world, but be transformed by the renewing of your mind. Then you will be able to test and approve what God's will is—his good, pleasing and perfect will** (Romans 12:1-2 NIV, emphasis mine).

The great thing about hanging out with God, being mentored by Him, and having Him renew our minds and mature our thinking, is that gaining His best perspective for us will positively affect the rest of our lives.

It is not surprising that God Himself recommends that we learn from

Him. We can see this in the following passage.

> Jesus said, "Come to me, all of you who are weary and carry heavy burdens, and I will give you rest. Take my yoke upon you. **Let me teach you,** because I am humble and gentle, and you will find rest for your souls. For my yoke fits perfectly, and the burden I give you is light" (Matthew 11:28-30, emphasis mine).

There are many reasons why it is of great value for each of us to learn from God—many more than I could write in this book or than I even know about. But learning from God is of great value and something I want to do in my own life. When I first entered into a relationship with God, I realized that there were many different religions and philosophies in our world. Early on, I committed to learn from God and asked Him to help me understand what is the truth. This became my ongoing request to God over the years, that He would teach me every day of my life, and that I would know truth in my inner being. If you haven't done so already, I hope you would join me and ask God to do the same for you.

The Tremendous Privilege It Is to Learn From God

People count it a privilege to meet the president of a country, a movie star, or a famous athlete. How much greater is it to meet the Creator of the universe—the One to whom we owe our very existence! I like to ponder God's greatness, although I cannot truly begin to fathom it. I have enjoyed thinking about the following verses.

> The LORD is exalted over all the nations, his glory above the heavens. Who is like the LORD our God, the One who sits enthroned on high, **who stoops down to look on the heavens and the earth**? (Psalm 113:4-6 NIV, emphasis mine)

If God is so great that it requires humility on His part to stoop down to look upon the heavens and the earth, how much farther does He have to humble Himself to be with us? And yet God loves us so much that He is willing to be intimately familiar with us in great detail. We can see this in the following verses:

> O LORD, **you have examined my heart and know everything about me.** You know when I sit down or stand up. You know my every thought when far away. You chart the path ahead of me and tell me where to stop and rest. Every moment you know where I am. You know what I am going to say even before I say it, LORD. You both precede and follow me. You place your hand of blessing on my head. Such knowledge is too wonderful for me, too great for me to know! I can never escape from your spirit! I can never get away from your presence! If I go up to heaven, you are there; if I go down to the place of the dead, you are there. If I ride the wings of the morning, if I dwell by the farthest oceans, even there your hand will guide me, and your strength will support me. I could ask the darkness to hide me and the light around me to become night—but even in darkness I cannot hide from you. To you the night shines as bright as day. Darkness and light are both alike to you. You made all the delicate, inner parts of my body and knit me together in my mother's womb. Thank you for making me so wonderfully complex! Your workmanship is marvelous—and how well I know it. You watched me as I was being formed in utter seclusion, as I was woven together in the dark of the womb. You saw me before I was born. Every day of my life was recorded in your book. Every moment was laid out before a single day had passed. How precious are your thoughts about me, O God! They are innumerable! I can't even count them; they outnumber the grains of sand! **And when I wake up in the morning, you are still with me!** (Psalm 139:1-18, emphasis mine)

It is a great privilege to learn from the One who always loves us, is always with us, and knows everything about us—the One who knows us better than we know ourselves!

It is also a privilege to learn from the One who knows exactly what is best for us to learn. The following verses demonstrate how people loved to learn from Jesus (God), because He completely knew what He was talking about.

> After Jesus finished speaking, the crowds were amazed at his teaching, for he taught as one who had real authority—quite unlike the teachers of religious law (Matthew 7:18-29).

> All the people hung on every word he said (Luke 19:48).

It is encouraging to know that God knows exactly what He is doing in our lives. This is certainly a contrast to being taught by someone who is only trying out their latest theories on us. God is definitely the #1 instructor of all time, with the #1 curriculum plan tailored uniquely to each of us for our very best!

Chapter 3 – Practical Ways To Learn From God

Now that we have examined the importance of learning from God and why it is a tremendous privilege to do so, we now turn to the question: "How can we actually learn from God?"

PAUSE POINT

This is our first pause point in this book. I'll place these pause points throughout the book as places for you to contemplate your answers to a question or two, before I dive into some of my thoughts on a topic. If you first explore your thoughts on a topic, through a pause-point question, it may help you to think more about the issues and thus create a more meaningful reading experience for you. So, if this approach sounds good to you, please take a moment to ponder the following question before continuing to read.

How do you go about learning from God in your own life?

If you were to ask me this question, I would likely answer by starting with the following passage from the Bible:

> But you have received the Holy Spirit, and he lives within you, so you don't need anyone to teach you what is true. For the Spirit teaches you all things, and what he teaches is true—it is not a lie. So continue in what he has taught you, and continue to live in Christ (1 John 2:27).

When we received forgiveness because of Jesus' work on the cross, and we in turn invited God into our hearts, God's Spirit came to live inside of us and began to teach us from within. But how does this actually take place? I'll list some of the ways with which I am familiar.

God Is a Filter

God's Spirit within us is like a filter. A filter is often used to strain out impurities from a liquid. In a similar way, our senses provide information to us by what we see, hear, and feel. As this various sensory data comes to us, God on the inside of us will act as a filter to give us the sense of which thoughts are good for us to keep, and which thoughts would be best to strain out.

Sometimes when I read or listen to something, it doesn't ring true to me. I might not be able to put my finger on what exactly wasn't right, but God within me was pointing out that something was wrong. In doing this, God helps to strain out that which isn't good for me. In some of these cases, I later learned more from God and realized what part of the statement was actually good (or at least acceptable), and what part was bad and needed to be strained out. But at the time of the initial filtering, it was good enough to just have the whole thing strained out. It is like taking a bite of apple and sensing something doesn't taste quite right. After spitting out the bad bite, it becomes apparent that there is a worm in the apple. "Learning more" is done by taking a knife and cutting up the apple. Once the part affected by the worm is removed, the rest of the apple can be quite good to eat.

God inside of us works as more than just a filter, however. He also enhances and gives insights into the data we receive. As we read or hear something, we might suddenly have an insight about it. This might be as simple as an idea dawning on us: "Oh, how about that! I didn't realize that before." Or it might be an "ah-ha" moment, in which something suddenly stands out to us and we realize it is quite significant.

God inside of us also enhances our conscience. In my own life, before I entered into a relationship with God, my sense of morality was primarily based upon the benefit I thought I would gain in doing something, versus the likelihood of and the penalty involved in getting caught. But when God came inside of me, I became much more aware of what things were good to do and what things were best to avoid.

Besides enhancing our conscience, God also enhances our common sense. He does this partly by enriching our speech and our knowledge (1 Corinthians 1:4-6). God also renews our minds and gives us a better sense of what things are practical, good to do, and pleasing to Him (Romans 12:1-2).

God works in all of us who have entered into a relationship with Him. He teaches us, causes us to grow, and helps us to think better as He filters and enhances the data we receive, our conscience, and common sense. But God can also bring very direct or extraordinary insight into our circumstances. We can see this in the following verses:

> Then after I have poured out my rains again, I will pour out my Spirit upon all people. Your sons and daughters will prophesy. Your old men will dream dreams. Your young men will see visions. In those days, I will pour out my Spirit even on servants, men and women alike (Joel 2:28-29).

Sometimes God communicates in ways that are even more direct than visions or dreams. For example, in Exodus 33:11 God spoke face to face with Moses, in the same manner that a man would speak to his friend. It doesn't get much more direct than that!

These more direct forms of communication are less common than the filtering, conscience, and common sense God usually brings to our lives. For example, I have seen God teach me almost every day in these common ways. But on occasion, I have experienced more direct insight, such as the day I went to look for an apartment in a town close to where my fiancée lived. That morning, I was reading the Bible and suddenly I knew deep inside myself that the apartment I would rent would cost $250 a month. (You can probably tell from this price that this was some time ago, back in 1983!) I looked at many apartments that day, but none were renting for that exact price. When I almost ran out of time to look, I began to wonder if I had "heard" the price correctly. I kept praying for God to guide me, and as I was driving down a certain road, I suddenly felt that I shouldn't go any farther. I pulled my car over to the side of the road, but I was confused—I could not see any apartments from where I was parked. My fiancée was with me, and she had seen an "apartment-for-rent" sign on the previous block. I called and found that they indeed had an apartment for $250.

This was the first time I experienced such specific guidance from God. But there are many people who are in relationship with God who receive little or no direct guidance from Him. However, whether with extraordinary forms of guidance or none at all, I'm glad that God guides us through His filtering, our conscience, and our common sense, and that He can also give us more direct forms of guidance when He knows it is best to give it.

What Can We Do on Our Part?

It's great having the God of the universe living inside of us, guiding us, and teaching us the things that are good for us to know. But besides paying attention to His instruction, is there anything else we can do to help in this process? The following are some of the things I have found helpful to do.

1. Ask God to help our hearts be good soil for learning.

2. Take time to read the Bible. This is one of the excellent sources that God can use in teaching us.

3. Look to God for wisdom wherever we lack it.

Let's take a look at each of these three items.

Being Good Heart Soil

One thing we can do is ask God for soft hearts that can easily receive those things He is trying to teach us. This was the "good soil" in the parable of the seeds (which we looked at in Chapter 1).

> The good soil represents the hearts of those who truly accept
> God's message and produce a huge harvest—thirty, sixty, or
> even a hundred times as much as had been planted (Matthew
> 13:23).

This good soil was soft enough to receive the seed well, but the
harder soil could not receive the seed.

> For the hearts of these people are hardened, and their ears
> cannot hear, and they have closed their eyes—so their eyes
> cannot see, and their ears cannot hear, and their hearts cannot
> understand, and they cannot turn to me and let me heal them
> (Matthew 13:15).

There is a quick and sure way to hinder our ability to learn from God:
All we have to do is harden our hearts and not receive what He is
teaching us. It is like a parent who is talking to a child but the child
puts their fingers in their ears so that they can't hear. At one point,
Jesus was instructing His disciples and saw that their hearts were
becoming hardened. This is what Jesus shared with them:

> Jesus knew what they were thinking, so he said, "Why are you
> so worried about having no food? **Won't you ever learn or
> understand? Are your hearts too hard to take it in?**" (Mark
> 8:17, emphasis mine).

These verses show the relationship between having a hardened heart
and not being able to learn or understand. If we harden our hearts, we
can quickly stop the great things God wants to do in our lives. For this
reason, God gives us the following strong warning for our benefit:

> But never forget the warning: "Today you must listen to his
> voice. Don't harden your hearts against him as Israel did when
> they rebelled" (Hebrews 3:15).

But if we have soft hearts, God can grant us wisdom, knowledge, and understanding, as the following verses indicate:

> For the LORD grants wisdom! From his mouth come knowledge and understanding (Proverbs 2:6).

> **For wisdom will enter your heart,** and knowledge will fill you with joy (Proverbs 2:10, emphasis mine).

The Bible As an Excellent Source

Something else we can do on our part to learn from God is to spend time reading His Word.

The Bible is a wonderful book that God has written through people who were in a strong relationship with Him. It contains an incredible amount of great instruction for us.

We can get even more out of what we read in the Bible if we ask God to always teach us when we read, and if we then pay special attention to those things that stand out to us. As I said earlier, God inside of us works as more than just as a filter. He will also enhance and give insights into the different data we receive. As we read or hear something, we might suddenly receive an insight into it. I have found that God does this by making certain things stand out to me when I read the Bible. It is as if the text suddenly becomes set in boldface type or highlighted, even though it is really not. It is hard to describe, but if you have experienced it, then you know exactly what I am saying. If you have not experienced this yet, you may want to ask God to help you do so.

As I'm reading the Bible, when something really stands out to me, I'll pause to look at it, and I am often amazed at how it pertains to something I'm going through, or how it answers a question in my mind. This is even more amazing to me when I think of all the verses I've read over the years and how I always seem to read the one that

AT HIS FEET | 229

is just right for that particular time in my life. It is mind-boggling to ponder how many details God must be using to teach me. By causing certain things to stand out to each of us, God tailors the Bible uniquely to our lives. However, there are still questions we will face in life to which we won't find direct answers in the Bible, such as what job we should take, where we should live, and exactly how we should be spending our time and money. In these situations, I find it very helpful to ask God for wisdom.

God's Wisdom As an Excellent Source

Earlier, we looked at a verse in Proverbs 2 that tells how God can bring wisdom into our hearts. If we look at a larger section of this chapter, of which this verse is a part, we will learn more about the importance of wisdom.

> Tune your ears to wisdom, and concentrate on understanding. Cry out for insight and understanding. Search for them as you would for lost money or hidden treasure. Then you will understand what it means to fear the LORD, and you will gain knowledge of God. For the LORD grants wisdom! From his mouth come knowledge and understanding. He grants a treasure of good sense to the godly. He is their shield, protecting those who walk with integrity. He guards the paths of justice and protects those who are faithful to him.
>
> Then you will understand what is right, just, and fair, and you will know how to find the right course of action every time. For wisdom will enter your heart, and knowledge will fill you with joy. Wise planning will watch over you. Understanding will keep you safe.
>
> Wisdom will save you from evil people, from those whose speech is corrupt (Proverbs 2:2-12).

It is good for us to tune our ears to God's wisdom! His wisdom is so important that we should seek it as if we were searching for lost money or hidden treasure.

Life is so much more difficult to navigate without God's wisdom. I have faced numerous situations as a husband, parent, friend, and employee in which I did not know what was the best thing to do. But when I eventually turned to God and asked for His wisdom, He helped me greatly in these situations. Through these experiences, I have become very fond of the following verses that tell us that anytime we are lacking in wisdom, we should ask God for His wisdom and He will graciously grant our request.

> **If you need wisdom—if you want to know what God wants you to do—ask him, and he will gladly tell you. He will not resent your asking.** But when you ask him, be sure that you really expect him to answer, for a doubtful mind is as unsettled as a wave of the sea that is driven and tossed by the wind. People like that should not expect to receive anything from the Lord. They can't make up their minds. They waver back and forth in everything they do (James 1:5-8, emphasis mine).

I've been asking God for wisdom a lot more lately, and He is helping me to notice more quickly the gap between what I know and what would be good for me to know. Many times in the past I have felt inadequate for not knowing what to do in a situation. I have thought, *What is wrong with me? Shouldn't I know what to do here?* I have especially felt tempted to think this way when the situation didn't actually seem to be large or difficult. I'm thankful that these verses from James give me the freedom and encouragement to ask God for wisdom, no matter how small the problem might be.

Sometimes my lack of wisdom results from my not knowing the future and being faced with a decision in which such knowledge could really be useful. But I have found in these situations that just a little bit of guidance from God can go a long way. If God grants me the wisdom to know what is His best for me to do, then it definitely solves any "tiebreakers" between possible choices! It also provides an anchor for any future doubts, because even in difficult times it is easier to be at peace when I am certain that I have chosen God's best for me. When I was thinking of getting married, I desired God's guidance. I knew that there were many unforeseen variables in marriage, and I only wanted to take that step if it was God's best for me. So I asked God for wisdom and then waited for the needed confirmation from Him. When I received the "green light," so to speak, it provided a strong foundation to my married life because I was certain that getting married was what God had wanted me to do.

As I have asked God for wisdom at different times over the years, I have been amazed at His ability to provide what I have needed. Many times I have asked God for wisdom and a few months later realized that I somehow had the wisdom and understanding that I had lacked earlier. At times I could trace the exact point at which the wisdom arrived, such as through something someone said, something I read in the Bible, or even something that dawned on me as I was cutting the grass! But at other times, I had no idea how God gave me the understanding of what was best to do. Maybe I just wasn't paying attention, or perhaps He provided it just below my level of consciousness. In either case, it is amazing the incredible number of details God uses to provide what is needed.

In the following passage from James, I have wondered at times why the qualification exists that the person must expect an answer and not have a doubtful mind.

> If you need wisdom—if you want to know what God wants you to do—ask him, and he will gladly tell you. He will not resent your asking. **But when you ask him, be sure that you really expect him to answer, for a doubtful mind is as unsettled as a wave of the sea that is driven and tossed by the wind. People like that should not expect to receive anything from the Lord. They can't make up their minds. They waver back and forth in everything they do** (James 1:5-8,

emphasis mine).

I'm not sure what the full answer is, but I do know that if we ask God for wisdom but don't trust Him to bring the answer in His way and time, we might be tempted to run ahead and not wait for God. The Bible describes many situations in which people did not ask God for His wisdom or did not wait for Him to bring the needed understanding. In these instances, the bad effects of the poor decisions that they made become obvious. There is a trust factor that is needed—trust that God will indeed bring in the needed insight in His way and time. This reminds me of the following verses that show the value of keeping in step with God.

> If we are living now by the Holy Spirit, let us follow the Holy Spirit's leading in every part of our lives (Galatians 5:25).

> O Israel, how can you say the LORD does not see your troubles? How can you say God refuses to hear your case? Have you never heard or understood? Don't you know that the LORD is the everlasting God, the Creator of all the earth? He never grows faint or weary. No one can measure the depths of his understanding.

> He gives power to those who are tired and worn out; he offers strength to the weak. Even youths will become exhausted, and young men will give up. **But those who wait on the LORD will find new strength. They will fly high on wings like eagles. They will run and not grow weary. They will walk and not faint** (Isaiah 40:27-31, emphasis mine).

God's altar can bring freedom to our lives. But it is important for us to look to God for wisdom at the altar, or we could easily sacrifice the wrong things there. With our ability to harden our hearts and rationalize our behavior, it is easy to give God a substitute for what He is asking us to do. For example, we might get very busy doing many "good" activities for Him, but miss the most important thing we could do: get to know Him. The foolish bridesmaids seemed to have this dilemma. The bridesmaids who did well were the ones who had acquired wisdom. Therefore, I think it is wise to share our full hearts' desires with God, surrender all of our desires on the altar, and attain wisdom from God as to what is best to sacrifice or to keep.

Practical Things We Can Do

In this final section, I would like to sum up and extend some of the practical aspects in this chapter. I have personally found all of these things to be very helpful for me to do. At the same time, I realize they may fit into your life somewhat differently than they do into mine. So I welcome you to join me in asking God to give us wisdom to see how these things can best fit into our lives.

> **1.** Ask God for a soft heart and a willingness to follow His best for us.
>
> Ultimately, the needed ability to learn from God comes from God. Asking God for this ability is a great thing for us to do.
>
> **2.** Ask God to teach us through all of life and take time to read the Bible daily.
>
> I would highly recommend that we ask God to teach us through all of life, including what we read in the Bible. When we read the Bible, God can make certain things stand out to us, and if we pause and contemplate those things, we will be amazed at how God causes those things to pertain to what we are currently going through in our daily lives.
>
> If you have never read the Bible before, I would recommend reading the book of John first and then the entire New Testament. In order to stay consistent, I would read at least one chapter a day. God has packed the Bible with a tremendous amount of wisdom. It is like an iceberg that, at

first glance, does not seem large until we understand what lies beneath the surface of the water. Each time you read through the Bible with God teaching you, you'll be amazed at how much more is below the surface. My favorite Bible translations are the New International Version and the New Living Translation. You can find these at almost any Christian bookstore. If you would like additional ideas on how to read and study the Bible, please see the appendix of this book.

3. Seek wisdom wherever we need it.

Any time we notice a gap between what we know and what would seem good for us to know, it is good for us to ask God for the needed wisdom. For those requests that take longer to be answered, we could write down what we ask for and then mark a date on our calendars a few months later for us to review those requests. When we review our lists, we may want to ask ourselves the following questions:

~ Am I amazed at what I now know in regard to my requests?

~ Do I know how God had me attain the needed insights?

Summary

This chapter was written to help us focus on how to learn from God. Even though we can't sit physically at Jesus' feet today as Mary did, we instead have the tremendous privilege of having His Holy Spirit dwell within us and teach us from the inside. Being able to learn from God, like Mary did, is a tremendous privilege that is key to our growing in His very best for us.

Chapter 4 – Friendship With God

A high-school boy and girl fell in love for the first time. Many of their thoughts are consumed with how wonderful the other person is. When asked why they like the other person so much or what they think is so great about the other person, they may struggle to communicate clearly all of the wonderful thoughts that have permeated their minds. It's as if they have pictures in their minds of each other that are wonderful but hard to describe. As the saying goes, "A picture is worth a thousand words."

In a similar way, the heart of a deep friendship with God is a love relationship that goes beyond words. Mary had this kind of love in her heart for Jesus, which in turn gave her a strong desire to stay at His feet. If she did not have this love in her heart, I doubt she would have been so motivated to be with Him.

In this chapter, we'll explore the topic of a deep love-friendship with God. We'll do this in three main sections:

   1. Some overall thoughts about friendship with God

   2. How we can grow in friendship with God

   3. Practical things we can do

SECTION 1 – Overall Thoughts About Friendship With God

   And we know that the Son of God has come, and he has given us understanding so that we can know the true God…(1 John 5:20).

   You love him even though you have never seen him… (1 Peter 1:8).

To know and love God in a deep friendship is my highest goal in life.

God is the best friend I could ever have, and I certainly would like for God to consider me a very close friend of His. So, this chapter on friendship with God is very near and dear to my heart. I hope that as I share my passion about this wonderful topic, you will find it of value to you in your walk with God, just as I have in mine.

Falling in Love

When I think about the high-school boy and girl that fell in love, it reminds me of my own relationship with God. Like the high-school couple, I also have wonderful thoughts in my mind about God. The high-school boy and girl will eventually begin to realize that the other has faults. But I am thankful that God is more wonderful than I know, and that the more I get to know Him, the more amazing I find Him to be! I can only scratch the surface of how wonderful He is! I am so glad that God has designed us for deep, lasting relationships with Him, and that there is no better thing He could give us than eternal friendship with Himself.

Focusing on Jesus

In my friendship with God, I find it very helpful to focus on Jesus, because He provides me with a personal contact point from which to interact with an infinite God. In Colossians 1:15, Paul wrote that Jesus is the visible image of the invisible God. So, instead of trying to relate to a huge invisible God, I am thankful that God came to the earth in the person of Jesus—Someone to whom I can very much relate. As I read in the Bible how Jesus interacted with different people, I better understand who God is. The Scriptures reveal His desires and show how He relates to people.

If someone would say to me, "Shouldn't you focus on God the Father instead of Jesus?" I would answer, "If your life with God works well that way, great! But I personally like to focus on Jesus because He provides me with a personal point of contact with God. I also know that if I have friendship with the Son (Jesus), I have friendship with the

Father, as well." The following verses show this relationship.

> Jesus said, "Anyone who denies the Son doesn't have the Father either. But anyone who confesses the Son has the Father also" (1 John 2:23).

> "Where is your father?" they asked. Jesus answered, "Since you don't know who I am, you don't know who my Father is. If you knew me, then you would know my Father, too" (John 8:19).

The following analogy is helpful in seeing how Jesus can be our personal point of contact with God. It also shows the relationship between the three parts of God (the Father, the Son [Jesus], and the Holy Spirit) but how they are all one God.

When I turn on the kitchen faucet, water keeps pouring and pouring out of it until I turn it off. How can so much water come out of such a small faucet? Because there is a whole reservoir of water behind that faucet! When we look at God, the Father is like the reservoir, the Son (Jesus) is like the faucet (the part out of which we see the water flowing), and the Holy Spirit is like the water that fills our cups. We are the cups that contain the water of God's Holy Spirit within us. God is like the water in the sense that the water is still water no matter where it is at, whether it's in the reservoir, coming out of the faucet, or in the cups. But when I walk up to the sink, the first thing I see is the faucet out of which the water is flowing, and that's my focal point for interacting with God.

Even though I find this analogy to be helpful, it quickly breaks down by not showing the perfect relationship that God has with Himself, as all three parts interact in a perfect love-friendship. God's friendship with Himself is so complete that God is not in need of our friendship, and yet in His great love for us, He invites us to join into this wonderful friendship that He has with Himself.

Now that I have explained why Jesus is the focal point of my heart in relating with an infinite God, it will make it easier for me to communicate personally about God by predominantly referring to Him as "Jesus" instead of "God" throughout the rest of this book.

Jesus As a Best Friend

PAUSE POINT

> Why do you think Jesus is the best Friend that you or I could ever have?

When I look at friendship with God, I think, *What qualities does Jesus have that make Him a better friend than anyone else?* The following four points are a good start toward answering this question.

1) Jesus loves us perfectly.

Jesus loves me perfectly all the time. The consistency of His love is amazing! I have often looked to humans to love me consistently, and in turn, I have often been sorely disappointed. But Jesus has never faltered in His love for me. When I consider Jesus hanging on the cross paying for my sins, knowing that He could come down from the cross at any time, and yet He was willing to take all of my punishment upon Himself, I think, *Wow, what a demonstration of His amazing love for me! There is no one else who loves me like that!*

> Jesus said, "The greatest love is shown when people lay down their lives for their friends" (John 15:13).

> When we were utterly helpless, Christ [Jesus] came at just the right time and died for us sinners. Now, no one is likely to die for a good person, though someone might be willing to die for a person who is especially good. But God showed his great love for us by sending Christ [Jesus] to die for us while we were still sinners (Romans 5:6-8).

It is amazing that even when I was hostile and unloving toward God in my atheistic childhood, He had still lovingly laid down His life for me. When I had no way to attain His love, He loved me anyway and was willing to ransom me from the penalties I deserved. Jesus rescued me from those negative aspects of myself that kept me from a relationship with Him, and He continues to daily free me to walk in love and friendship with Him. I'm glad for Jesus' perfect love and for His constancy in always having that love for me. Just knowing I'm so loved has brought stability to my life. Jesus' love is the safest place for our hearts to respond to His wonderful invitation to a deep friendship. In fact, it is the safest place for relationship, since Jesus will never hurt us in relationship as most humans will.

2) Jesus is always there for us and is willing to help us.

Jesus has the wonderful friendship quality of availability. If we are going through a hard time, will our friends always be there for us? If we are fortunate to have good friends, they might be there for us most of the time. But Jesus is there for us all of the time. Not only is His presence with us, but He also indwells us by His Holy Spirit. Talk about intimacy and closeness! When we first entered into relationship with Him, at the very point when we received Him, He literally took up residency within us. I'm glad that God is with us all the time!

Friends will lend a listening ear, but Jesus is with us 24-7 to listen to us share with Him those things that are troubling us or are on our minds. Not only is He there to listen, but He can also give us strength, insight, peace, and healing. I'm glad that when He listens to us, He not only cares and understands, but He does so perfectly and completely. The following verses speak about the care He has for us:

> Give all your worries and cares to God, for he cares about what happens to you (1 Peter 5:7).

> Don't worry about anything; instead, pray about everything. Tell God what you need, and thank him for all he has done. If

you do this, you will experience God's peace, which is far more wonderful than the human mind can understand. His peace will guard your hearts and minds as you live in Christ Jesus (Philippians 4:6-7).

3) Jesus is never a "jerk."

All of us have the capability of being a "jerk!" There are times when we become stressed and tired and are irritable toward others and treat them in ways we wouldn't want to be treated. Unlike us, Jesus will never be a jerk. He doesn't become tired and irritable. He won't go from being in a good mood and accepting us to quickly changing to a bad mood and then rejecting us. Instead, He has unconditional love toward us all the time. I'm glad that Jesus is always a solid and consistent Friend. Jesus is definitely the rock of my relationship with Him!

I like the following Scripture passage because it speaks of Jesus' consistency.

> Have you never heard or understood? Don't you know that the LORD is the everlasting God, the Creator of all the earth? **He never grows faint or weary.** No one can measure the depths of his understanding. He gives power to those who are tired and worn out; he offers strength to the weak. Even youths will become exhausted, and young men will give up. But those who wait on the LORD will find new strength. They will fly high on wings like eagles. They will run and not grow weary. They will walk and not faint (Isaiah 40:28-31, emphasis mine).

4) Jesus is the most personal Friend.

Jesus is the most personal Friend we could ever have. If we open our hearts wide to Him, He won't act like some humans do and suddenly begin to take us for granted, try to use us, or treat us badly. Instead, as we open our hearts wider to Him, we'll find that He has already been at that deeper level and will fully meet us in a heart-to-heart friendship there. It is fascinating that we are the ones who are limited in how far we can go in relationship with Him, but Jesus is not limited in His relationship with us. We have a totally safe place to fully open wide our hearts, a place to share all of our desires and concerns, a place where it is safe to live with the best possible Friend, Jesus.

Even though Jesus is my best Friend, I treat my relationship with Him with tremendous respect. I realize that although Jesus is the best Friend I will ever have, He is also the God of the universe—a God who is awesome, powerful, and holy. Therefore, interacting with Jesus is a little bit like interacting with electricity. If I am dealing with high voltage, I definitely want to be insulated! In the Old Testament, David learned this lesson the hard way when his friend Uzzah touched the ark of God and was struck dead instantly. This event frightened David, but it also caused him to have an even greater respect for God.

> But when they arrived at the threshing floor of Nacon, the oxen stumbled, and Uzzah put out his hand to steady the Ark of God. Then the LORD's anger blazed out against Uzzah for doing this, and God struck him dead beside the Ark of God.

> David was now afraid of the LORD and asked, "How can I ever bring the Ark of the LORD back into my care?" So David decided not to move the Ark of the LORD into the City of David. He took it instead to the home of Obed-edom of Gath. The Ark of the LORD remained there with the family of Obed-edom for three months, and the LORD blessed him and his entire household.

> Then King David was told, "The LORD has blessed Obed-edom's home and everything he has because of the Ark of God." So David went there and brought the Ark to the City of David with a great celebration. After the men who were carrying it had gone six steps, they stopped and waited so David could sacrifice an ox and a fattened calf. And David

danced before the LORD with all his might, wearing a priestly tunic. So David and all Israel brought up the Ark of the LORD with much shouting and blowing of trumpets (2 Samuel 6:6-7, 9-15).

The first time I read this passage, I was shocked by it. Had God maintained His perfect quality of love at the point when He struck Uzzah dead? Now I realize that I was looking at the wrong side of the coin. On the one side of the coin, God was perfectly maintaining His love, as He always does. But on the other side of the coin, His tremendous holiness is so great that no one can approach Him without being properly insulated by His forgiveness through the blood He shed on the cross.

At times, God's perfect holiness is hard for me to grasp. Jesus' perfection and greatness are too much for my small human brain to comprehend. When John the Baptist encountered Jesus, he sensed Jesus' greatness and concluded that he himself was not even worthy to be Jesus' servant or carry His sandals. This Jesus is the One to whom we owe our very existence—as well as the existence of the entire universe! He is so great that we don't even deserve to carry His sandals for Him. And yet, if we approach Him in humility (and in light of His payment on the cross), Jesus says that He desires to gather us to Himself as a mother hen gathers her chicks under her wings. (See Matthew 23:37.)

This is the kind of intimacy that God would like to have with us—He wants us to be close to His heart. But again, the context must be that we approach God from a place of being "insulated." For example, I love drawing close to Jesus, but I always do so with an attitude of reverence and in acknowledgement of His tremendous power. Christ can do as He pleases, and I do not take lightly His mercy toward me. But I also know that I can be close to Him because of His blood that was shed for me on the cross. So, I look to Jesus to help me keep from being judgmental, angry, or manipulative toward Him. Instead I hope to care for Jesus as He does for me: I desire to be an excellent friend to Him.

More Than a Celebrity

People often get excited when they see someone famous. If they actually get to meet the person, their excitement level may skyrocket. But consider how much greater is the privilege of having your best Friend be the God of the universe! The One who is all powerful, totally loving, and the most wonderful Friend that I could ever have is the Creator of all things!

People often do not fully realize how important or valuable another person is to them until that person dies. At the funeral, they often regret not having told the person how much they valued and appreciated them. In a similar way, because Jesus is always with us, it is easy to under-appreciate Him. I wonder, *How would I feel if this were the last day that Jesus would ever be alive? What would I want to say to Him? How would I feel at the thought of having to live life without Him being with me all the time?*

PAUSE POINT

> If Jesus were only to be around for the rest of today, what would you want to tell Him?

Side note: In being limited to one-way communication in this book, I miss out on hearing your thoughts on what I've been writing. I would especially love to hear your response to this Pause Point. (It would be great if we could both take a few minutes to write down our answers. I would enjoy hearing yours, and then I could share with you…)

Here is what I would say to Him:

> I am so thankful for You, Jesus. Thank You for being my best Friend and for always being with me. Thank You for teaching me and helping me to grow in Your love and friendship

qualities. I sure am going to miss You tremendously!

I am very thankful that Jesus will never die and that He will never cease being my best Friend! Every year I find my appreciation of Him growing more and more in my heart, both for who He is and for the things He does. I'm thankful that the more I get to know Him, the more wonderful I find Him to be!

Knowing and Loving Jesus

I've asked Jesus a number of times to help me in the writing of this chapter. It is truly the "diamond" of this book in that it points to the greatest focus that we could ever have in life: to know and love Jesus. If this is the focus of your life, then I am excited for you, because with such a wonderful focus, not only do you have the best (Jesus), but I know He will also bring good things to the entirety of your life.

I'd like to end this section with a few Bible passages that point to the value of knowing and loving Jesus. Instead of putting my comments before each passage, as I typically do, I'll first give you the chance to read the passage and see what stands out to you. I'll then share those things that stand out to me, especially from the emphasized portions. The first of these passages is the main scripture upon which this book is based.

> As Jesus and the disciples continued on their way to Jerusalem, they came to a village where a woman named Martha welcomed them into her home. Her sister, **Mary, sat at the Lord's feet, listening to what he taught.** But Martha was worrying over the big dinner she was preparing. She came to Jesus and said, "Lord, doesn't it seem unfair to you that my sister just sits here while I do all the work? Tell her to come and help me."
>
> But the Lord said to her, "My dear Martha, you are so upset over all these details! **There is really only one thing worth**

being concerned about. Mary has discovered it—and I won't take it away from her" (Luke 10:38-42, emphasis mine).

I really like how Jesus affirmed Mary's focus on being with Him and listening to what He had to say. As I said earlier, these verses provide us with keys to get to know, learn from, and love Jesus even more.

> When Jesus had finished saying all these things, he looked up to heaven and said, "Father, the time has come. Glorify your Son so he can give glory back to you. For you have given him authority over everyone in all the earth. He gives eternal life to each one you have given him. **And this is the way to have eternal life—to know you, the only true God, and Jesus Christ, the one you sent to earth.** I brought glory to you here on earth by doing everything you told me to do. And now, Father, bring me into the glory we shared before the world began (John 17:1-5, emphasis mine).

> And we know that the Son of God has come, and he has given us understanding **so that we can know the true God.** And now we are in God because we are in his Son, Jesus Christ. He is the only true God, and he is eternal life (1 John 5:20, emphasis mine).

The very definition of eternal life focuses on getting to know God. In other parts of the Bible, this definition is expanded to include spending eternity with Jesus in heaven. But if friendship with Jesus is missed, then this main point is missed.

> One of the teachers of religious law was standing there listening to the discussion. He realized that Jesus had answered well, so he asked, "Of all the commandments, which is the most important?"

> Jesus replied, "**The most important commandment is this:**

'Hear, O Israel! The Lord our God is the one and only Lord. And you must love the Lord your God with all your heart, all your soul, all your mind, and all your strength.' The second is equally important: 'Love your neighbor as yourself.' No other commandment is greater than these" (Mark 12:28-31, emphasis mine).

The greatest commandment given to us—to love God—is not a burdensome law that is imposed on me. Instead, I see it as a tremendous privilege and freedom. It directs me to one of the most important elements needed for a good friendship with Jesus: having love in my heart for Him.

SECTION 2 – How We Can Grow in Friendship with God

Now that we have explored the overall topic of friendship with Jesus, let's take a look at several practical points on how we can actually grow in our friendship with Him.

1) Having an Open Heart Toward Jesus

In order to have a deep friendship with Jesus, one thing we need is an open heart. In Chapter 1, we looked at the parable of the seeds. The good soil was soft enough to receive the seed well. If we are going to have a heart-to-heart friendship with Jesus, then the soil of our heart needs to be soft and receptive to Him.

This concept also applies to human relationships. A certain amount of openness of heart is required for good relationships. In Paul's relationship with the Corinthians, he realized this key element was lacking.

Oh, dear Corinthian friends! We have spoken honestly with you. **Our hearts are open to you.** If there is a problem between us, it is not because of a lack of love on our part, but because you have withheld your love from us. I am talking now as I would to my own children. **Open your hearts to us!** (2 Corinthians 6:11-13, emphasis mine).

There are many concepts we understand from our human relationships, including the value of openness, that we can apply to our relationship with Jesus. I hope you find the following exercise helpful to see some of these correlations.

Exercise Scenario 1

Think of someone who has been hostile or critical toward you.

How do you feel about how this person has treated you?

Exercise Scenario 2

Now think of a person who has been outwardly friendly to you and even greets you with a smile, but internally they seem to stiff-arm you and keep you at a distance. They may be polite to you, but they do not really share themselves with you, nor are they interested in your sharing yourself with them. On the surface, this person seems to be "with" you, but in reality, they are far away.

How do you feel about how this person has treated you?

Exercise Scenario 3

Now think of a person who has not only been friendly to you, but who has also made time for you and listened to you. This person is willing to share their heart with you at a deep level. They also appreciate when you share your heart with them, and they listen carefully. This person does not try to one-up you but is kind to you. You count this person as your friend.

How do you feel about how this person has treated you?

Let's apply each of these scenarios to our friendship with Jesus.

Scenario 1:

If we treated Jesus the way the first person treated us, we would tend to be critical of God and hold things against Him. If we were really honest with ourselves, we would realize that we have actually had some very mean thoughts toward Him. Deep down, we really wouldn't think that God has our best interests in mind, and we would conclude that we would be better off keeping our distance from Him. Obviously, we wouldn't have much of a relationship with God.

Scenario 2:

If we treated Jesus the way the second person treated us, it might look like this: We would say our prayers and do "good" deeds, but we would never truly draw near to God in relationship. Instead, we would put up internal walls to keep God at arms' length. We would have bought into the deception that it is best to keep God from intruding upon our lives. We would think we'd be better off if we could "do our own thing" without God's guidance or interference. If we were really honest with ourselves, we would realize that our relationship with God consists of duty, but we are not that interested in friendship with Him.

Scenario 3:

If we treated Jesus the way the third person treated us, it might look like this: We would know Jesus as our best Friend. We would know that He only has good desires and intentions for us and that He loves us all the time. We would know that Jesus would never hurt us, and so we'd feel safe to draw near to Him and share the intimacy of our heart with Him. We would enjoy sitting at His feet in His presence. We would count on Him as our best Friend.

I hope your participation in this exercise has been helpful. I also hope that if we were to ask Jesus, "How do You feel about how we have treated You?" that He would reply that we have been His true friends.

One of the keys for us to grow in this type of relationship is to have an open heart toward Jesus. Asking Jesus to open our hearts to Him is one of the "how-to" keys to this treasure.

2) Inviting Jesus Into the Entirety of Our Lives and Everywhere We Go

Throughout this book, we have seen the importance of asking God to teach us in all of life. Similarly, it is also good to invite Jesus to go with us wherever we go. You might ask, "Isn't Jesus with us all of the time?" Technically He is, because He is always with us, but just because Jesus is with us does not mean we are with Him in relationship. It is like driving or walking somewhere with another person. Just because we are in close proximity to each other and even on the same route, we might not talk or even have a deep friendship with each other. It is completely different to truly go somewhere with another person when we are in a relationship with them. When a police officer takes a prisoner to jail, they go there together, but there is a good chance that the prisoner has a hostile attitude toward the police officer. In contrast, two people can take a trip together and deeply enjoy each other as they travel. I love to invite Jesus to go with me wherever I go. In the morning, I wake up and say, "Good morning, Jesus! I warmly invite You into my entire day and ask that You would help me to stay with You in my heart." At different times throughout the day, I invite Jesus to join me, such as when I go to work or to the store.

Moses felt the same way about being with Jesus. In Exodus 33, Moses told God that he only wanted to go to the Promised Land if God would go with him and the Israelites. If God didn't go with them, then Moses didn't want to take even a step in that direction. God was pleased with Moses and granted his request, because He knew him on a personal friendship level.

In this passage, we also find that Joshua liked to hang out in the Tent of Meeting, where God's presence was. It is no surprise that later in the Bible, Joshua is described as pleasing to God and doing well in God's best for him.

This desire to hang out with Jesus is captured nicely by a song written by Silverwind.

By His Spirit

I've heard stories of heaven, pavement made of gold.
Ageless beauty forever, that never grows old.
But if I got there only to find that, Jesus,
You were not up there…
Goodbye wings, angel things.

Heaven is being with You.
There's nothing I'd rather do.
There is nothing better, knowing You is heaven.
There is nothing better, loving You forever, Jesus.

Heaven holds only wishes, making dreams come true.
Heaven has to be Jesus, just being with You.
There is no laughter or joy in the music.
Jesus, if You are not there, then the song is all wrong.

Heaven is being with You.
There's nothing I'd rather do.
There is nothing better, knowing You is heaven.
There is nothing better, loving You forever, Jesus.[1]

Inviting Jesus into all of life and hanging out with Him in our hearts is key to growing in our friendship with Him.

3) Spending Quality Time with Jesus

One thing I find very helpful in my friendship with Jesus is to set aside time each day to spend alone with Him. Human friendships grow more deeply when people take quality time to talk with and enjoy each other, such as at mealtimes. Friendship can still take place when everyone is busy with cutting the grass, doing the laundry, and preparing meals. But being busy all the time without spending quality time together tends to take its toll on relationships. It's the same in our relationship with Jesus. It is good to invite Him to go with us wherever we go and ask Him to help us remain with Him in our hearts, but it is also important to spend quality time alone with Him in order for our friendship with Him to deepen.

In order to stay consistent, I find it helpful to set aside a certain time each day for me to be alone with Jesus. I try to be practical about this by picking a time when I can find a quiet place and am not likely to fall asleep. For me, this time works best right after my children go to bed. It is quieter and yet it is not immediately before I go to sleep. If I wait until right before I go to sleep, my time with Jesus may be too relaxing for me to stay awake!

During this time with Jesus, I usually read a few chapters of the Bible and pay special attention to those things that seem to stand out to me. When something does stand out, I pause and consider what it means. This is how Jesus often communicates with me—by causing His Word to stand out to me and helping me to understand how it pertains to my life. At some of these "pause points," I then communicate with Jesus by sharing what is on my heart with regard to the topic at hand. This includes sharing with Him my concerns or desires, or thanking Him for what the scripture passage has revealed about Him.

One of the great riches of the Bible is that it reveals who God is, what He desires, and how He relates to people. Just as I like to focus on Jesus as my personal contact point with an infinite God, I also like to focus on how He interacts with others. Although I've read the entire

Bible from cover to cover many times, I especially like to read the Gospels (Matthew, Mark, Luke, and John), paying special attention to how Jesus cares for and interacts with so many people. I really enjoy the accounts of His close friendships with people such as John, Mary, Martha, and Lazarus.

> After he had said this, Jesus was troubled in spirit and testified, "I tell you the truth, one of you is going to betray me." His disciples stared at one another, at a loss to know which of them he meant. One of them, **the disciple [John] whom Jesus loved, was reclining next to him.** Simon Peter motioned to this disciple and said, "Ask him which one he means." **Leaning back against Jesus,** he asked him, "Lord, who is it?" (John 13:21-25 NIV, emphasis mine).

> After he had said this, he went on to tell them, **"Our friend Lazarus has fallen asleep; but I am going there to wake him up."** His disciples replied, "Lord, if he sleeps, he will get better." Jesus had been speaking of his death, but his disciples thought he meant natural sleep (John 11:11-13, emphasis mine).

Note: The entire chapter of John 11 gives a wonderful account of Jesus' close friendship with Mary, Martha, and Lazarus. I won't repeat it here, but feel free to read it on your own if you are interested.

My quality time with Jesus is the part of my day I look forward to the most. I don't see this time as just reading a book (the Bible), but more as having a spiritual meal with God in which He makes the words come alive to my heart.

> Jesus said, "The Scriptures say, 'People need more than bread for their life; they must **feed on every word of God'"** (Matthew 4:4, emphasis mine).

Without food, the body becomes weak. Without spiritual food, the spirit becomes weak, and we lose our spiritual vitality and closeness with God. As Jesus makes His Word alive to my heart, it becomes a great strength to my life. I also just enjoy being with Him. That is why it is my favorite time of the day!

Having alone time with Jesus may work a little differently in your life than it does in mine. A different time might suit you better, such as your lunch break. You might find that crowded places work well for you, such as on a bus or train commute to and from work. You might go about reading the Bible differently or share your heart with Jesus differently than I do. But if you haven't done this before, I highly recommend it. It is more valuable than I could possibly describe. If you haven't done so already, you may want to ask Jesus to show you how to have consistent quality time with Him in your life. It is such a key to having a quality friendship with God.

4) Being with Jesus and Sharing Our Hearts With Him

My quality alone time with Jesus is a critical part of my friendship with Jesus, but aside from this time with Him, I like to "hang out" with Jesus at other times, as well. I enjoy silently basking in His presence. I sometimes do this when I find myself awake in the middle of the night, while I am driving to and from work, or on those rare days that I can start my day leisurely and spend extra time in bed just being in His presence. It is great to be able to spend time with a friend who loves me so completely.

After a time of silence, I often wind up naturally sharing with Jesus those things that seem to be on my mind or heart, just as I might do with a good human friend. This includes my deepest heart's desires and concerns.

David was a good friend of God's. God said that David was a man after His own heart—a nice compliment for David! David wrote in Psalm 62:

O my people, trust in him at all times. Pour out your heart to
him, for God is our refuge (Psalm 62:8).

Why would David encourage other people to pour out their hearts to
God? If Jesus already knows everything in our hearts, then why is
it good for us to share our hearts with Him? Jesus certainly doesn't
need to hear us say anything, does He? Because we know that Jesus
only wants our very best (because He completely loves us), then what
good things would He want to bring from our sharing our hearts with
Him?

PAUSE POINT

Do you have any ideas why Jesus would want us to pour our
hearts out to Him?

Part of the answer to this question can be found in human
relationships. If I have something on my mind that has been troubling
me, and if you are compassionate and have a good listening ear,
when I share with you, it can help to free me up. For starters, just by
sharing with you, I may realize more fully what has been troubling me.
And sometimes just acknowledging the fact that something is troubling
can be a step toward dealing with it. This sharing can also help to
build a deeper friendship between us. In a similar way, it is freeing
to share with Jesus what is on my heart and mind. It is wonderful to
share with the One who completely knows and loves me, and it helps
to grow my friendship with Him.

I like the following verses that encourage us to share our hearts with
Jesus. You may recognize these verses from earlier in this book.

Then Jesus said, "Come to me, all of you who are weary and
carry heavy burdens, and I will give you rest. Take my yoke
upon you. Let me teach you, because I am humble and gentle,
and you will find rest for your souls. For my yoke fits perfectly,
and the burden I give you is light" (Matthew 11:28-30).

Give all your worries and cares to God, for he cares about what happens to you (1 Peter 5:7, emphasis mine).

Don't worry about anything; instead, **pray about everything. Tell God what you need, and thank him for all he has done.** If you do this, you will **experience God's peace,** which is far more wonderful than the human mind can understand. His peace will guard your hearts and minds as you live in Christ Jesus (Philippians 4:6-7, emphasis mine).

It is wonderful that Jesus is willing to shoulder the burdens of our heart! He is willing for us to roll them onto Him. As I've done this at various times, I've noticed that after giving the burden to Him, different prayers will come into my heart, and I'll ask Jesus for His help or wisdom about those things that I have shared. This is an encouraging process, as He gives me peace in exchange for my burdens, and He gives me prayers that prove helpful over time.

Besides sharing my burdens, I also like to share my heart's desires with Jesus. For example, I might say, *Dear Jesus, I would really love to see a certain thing happen for myself or for someone else.* Or I might pray, *I ask for Your help with this certain thing.* Instead of trying to demand that Jesus take action, I simply give my desire to Him and ask Him to do what He would. In other words, I follow 1 Corinthians 13:5: Love does not demand its own way.

A friend of mine named Pam had an interesting experience a few months after she entered into a relationship with Jesus. Pam had shared with Jesus her desire that her son would help out more around the house. She didn't ask Jesus to do anything about it; she simply shared with Him the desire of her heart. A week or two later, her son asked if he could help clean the house, even though Pam had never talked with him about the situation. Pam's son was so diligent that he even lay on his back to vacuum the grill of the refrigerator! Later Pam remembered how she had shared her heart's desire with God, and she was amazed at what had occurred with her son.

Over the years I have shared many desires with Jesus and have seen Him bring about wonderful things, just like Pam. Other times I have shared with Him, but never saw Him make a change in that particular area. But whether Jesus brings about wonderful things or seemingly nothing, I trust that He knows the very best for my life. I also know that it is healthy for me to pour out my heart to Him, regardless of the outcome.

As I share my heart with Jesus, I try to be very honest with Him about my thoughts and feelings. If I hold back on being honest, I know it will only hinder me, but at the same time, I am careful with my honesty. I realize that like all of us, I can be tempted to judge Jesus or hold things against Him, just like I can be tempted to judge people and hold things against them. But to do so is a relational violation and does not treat Jesus as a Friend. I've heard some people claim that being angry with God is acceptable, and even that it is good to express your anger toward Him. Personally I do not think this is wise. Instead, it is better to identify such thoughts and feelings as being wrong, and to ask Jesus for forgiveness of such attitudes. Because the greatest thing I can do is to love God, when I share my heart with Him, I want to do so respectfully and with love toward Him. I want to treat Jesus with the same kind of love that He shows to me. But within this context, I find it very helpful to be honest with Him.

My desire is that Jesus would help us to enjoy His presence and that we would pour out our hearts to Him. This is an important key to our growing in friendship with Jesus. So, whether you know Jesus' presence in a great way or hardly at all, and whether or not sharing your heart with Him comes easy to you, I welcome you to join me in asking Jesus for the following things and then see what He is willing to do on your behalf.

> ~ Please help me to know You in a greater way and to just enjoy being with You.

> ~ Please help me to completely share my heart with You.

~ Please help me to be a good friend to You.

5) Having Our Hearts Cleansed

There are many things that can hinder our friendship with Jesus. In the parable of the seeds, we saw that there were thorns that grew up and hindered some of the plants from growing well. In the same way, there are many ways in which we can cause the soil of our hearts to not respond well to God in relationship.

Consider the following analogy: Our thoughts are like a stream that flows from our mind to our spiritual heart, which is like a pond. If we have bad thoughts, they will flow down the stream and contaminate the pond. If we harden our heart, even more pollution forms in the pond. Our spiritual eyes are at the bottom of our heart, and they look up through the pond toward Jesus. If the pond of our heart becomes polluted, it clouds the water and makes it difficult for us to see Him or sense His presence with us. Jesus described the important correlation between a "clean pond" and seeing Him, when He said, "God blesses those whose hearts are pure, for they will see God" (Matthew 5:8).

So, what do we do if our hearts are polluted? Fortunately, if we come before Jesus, ask Him to search us and show us if we have done anything wrong, confess those things to Him, and ask Him to forgive us based on His payment for us on the cross, then Jesus will not only clean out the pond of our heart, but He will also cleanse the stream of our mind, as well.

> This is the message he has given us to announce to you: God is light and there is no darkness in him at all. So we are lying if we say we have fellowship with God but go on living in spiritual darkness. We are not living in the truth. But if we are living in the light of God's presence, just as Christ is, then we have fellowship with each other, and the blood of Jesus, his Son, cleanses us from every sin. If we say we have no sin, we are only fooling ourselves and refusing to accept the truth.

But if we confess our sins to him, he is faithful and just to forgive us and to cleanse us from every wrong. If we claim we have not sinned, we are calling God a liar and showing that his word has no place in our hearts (1 John 1:5-10, emphasis mine).

In verse 9, the word "sin" is the Bible term for what I called "pollution" in the analogy. If we aren't willing to turn to God, and instead we hold onto sinful thoughts or desires, then they will isolate us from truly experiencing Jesus and His love for us. The Bible frequently emphasizes the importance of dealing with sin. If we don't deal with the sin in our lives, it will greatly hinder us from getting to know Jesus or be pleasing to Him.

So, what type of sin can pollute the pond? First John 2 provides a number of helpful examples.

My dear children, I am writing this to you so that you will not sin. But if you do sin, there is someone to plead for you before the Father. He is Jesus Christ, the one who pleases God completely. He is the sacrifice for our sins. He takes away not only our sins but the sins of all the world.

And how can we be sure that we belong to him? By obeying his commandments. If someone says, "I belong to God," but doesn't obey God's commandments, that person is a liar and does not live in the truth. But those who obey God's word really do love him. That is the way to know whether or not we live in him. Those who say they live in God should live their lives as Christ [Jesus] did.

Dear friends, I am not writing a new commandment, for it is an old one you have always had, right from the beginning. **This commandment—to love one another—**is the same message you heard before. Yet it is also new. This commandment is true in Christ and is true among you, because the darkness is disappearing and the true light is already shining.

> If anyone says, "I am living in the light," but hates a Christian brother or sister, that person is still living in darkness. Anyone who loves other Christians is living in the light and does not cause anyone to stumble. **Anyone who hates a Christian brother or sister is living and walking in darkness.** Such a person is lost, having been blinded by the darkness (1 John 2:1-11, emphasis mine).

Because the greatest commandments are to love God and to love our neighbors as ourselves, it is not surprising that any violation of love constitutes sin. If I judge someone, hold something against them, or even hate them, this is a relational violation of love, and it will, in turn, harm my relationship with Jesus. For my own sake, Jesus wants me to be free of such sins so that I can operate as I was designed to operate—to live life with His love flowing through me.

> Do not love the world or anything in the world. If anyone loves the world, the love of the Father is not in him. For everything in the world—**the cravings of sinful man, the lust of his eyes and the boasting of what he has and does**—comes not from the Father but from the world. The world and its desires pass away, but the man who does the will of God lives forever (1 John 2:15-17 NIV, emphasis mine).

If we become arrogant or lust after different things in our hearts, we pollute the pond. It is important for us to look to Jesus to help us think and desire only good things, but even in doing so, inevitably we will still sin. Therefore, it is good for the ponds of our hearts to be cleansed on a regular basis. I like to do this daily. Each morning, I ask Jesus if there is anything I've done wrong, and then I wait to see if He causes anything to stand out to me. If so, I confess these things, and ask Him to forgive me according to His payment for my sins on the cross. I then thank Jesus for His forgiveness. This process is another key to growing in friendship with Him.

6) Being Wholehearted

How would it have been if the high-school boy and girl that we looked at earlier in this chapter only had a slight desire to be together? Would their relationship look the same? Would they still have such wonderful thoughts about each other? Would they still look for any opportunity to be together?

In a similar way, to have a good friendship with Jesus we need to be wholehearted toward Him. If we lack this wholeheartedness, then other things in life will tend to crowd out our hearts and distract us from our "first love" for God. The importance of being wholehearted is seen in what Jesus stated as the greatest commandment:

> You must love the Lord your God **with all your heart,** all your soul, and all your mind (Matthew 22:37-38, emphasis mine).

If we hold back our hearts from Jesus, it is like pushing the brake in a car until it comes to a stop. A car is much easier to steer if it is moving; it is nearly impossible to steer if it is stopped. Instead of pushing the brake, if we have a warm heart toward Jesus and are wholehearted in following His best for us, then He can much more easily steer us in good directions for our lives.

Because Jesus only wants the best for us, if we are not wholehearted toward Him, it will only hinder the great things He wants to bring forth in our lives. Therefore, being wholehearted is one of the keys to pleasing Him. The following verses show how Jesus feels about those who are not wholehearted toward Him.

> Jesus said, **"I know all the things you do, that you are neither hot nor cold. I wish you were one or the other! But since you are like lukewarm water, I will spit you out of my mouth!** You say, 'I am rich. I have everything I want. I don't need a thing!' And you don't realize that you are wretched and miserable and poor and blind and naked. I advise you to buy

gold from me—gold that has been purified by fire. Then you will be rich. And also buy white garments so you will not be shamed by your nakedness. And buy ointment for your eyes so you will be able to see. I am the one who corrects and disciplines everyone I love. **Be diligent and turn from your indifference.**

"Look! Here I stand at the door and knock. If you hear me calling and open the door, I will come in, and we will share a meal as friends. I will invite everyone who is victorious to sit with me on my throne, just as I was victorious and sat with my Father on his throne. Anyone who is willing to hear should listen to the Spirit and understand what the Spirit is saying to the churches" (Revelation 3:15-22, emphasis mine).

Being wholehearted in following Jesus can keep us from making a common mistake: to substitute people for what only Jesus should predominantly be in our lives. If we do this, we will ultimately be disappointed with others because they cannot meet the deepest needs of our lives like Jesus can. For example, Jesus is the Source of love, and if our hearts are with Him first, then we will get "tanked up" with His perfectly constant love, and we will be able to have His love flow through our hearts to others. But if we first give our hearts to other people and look to them for perfect love, then we will surely be disappointed! We may even be tempted to manipulate other people to try to get them to love us more. So, when Jesus says that we should love God with our whole hearts, He is telling us how to have true freedom. Only if we truly love God first can we be in the place to have more of His love in our hearts for others.

So then, one of the keys to our growing in friendship with Jesus is to be wholehearted toward Him: to draw near to Him in our heart, have Him first in our heart, and have love in our heart for Him. If you have not already asked Jesus to help you with these things, then I welcome you to do so without hesitation.

Asking Jesus for these things solves a dilemma that I have had, and that a number of others have had, as well. There are times when I have felt a lack of desire to have Jesus first in my life. At these times, I've wondered what I should do, because without this in my heart, it seemed much harder to follow Him in all of His best for me. But then I read the following verses:

> So I advise you to live according to your new life in the Holy Spirit. Then you won't be doing what your sinful nature craves. The old sinful nature loves to do evil, which is just opposite from what the Holy Spirit wants. **And the Spirit gives us desires** that are opposite from what the sinful nature desires. These two forces are constantly fighting each other, and your choices are never free from this conflict. But when you are directed by the Holy Spirit, you are no longer subject to the law (Galatians 5:16-18, emphasis mine).

From these verses, I learned that Jesus can give us good desires through His Holy Spirit within us. So, when we feel that we are lacking good desires in our heart, we can ask Jesus to remove the bad desires from our heart and give us good desires instead.

7) Looking to Jesus to Build the Relationship

There is much more to friendship with Jesus than I've described in this chapter or even than I know! Looking to Jesus to build our relationship with Him, is probably the most important point of all, for in reality, I myself can't grow my relationship with God—only God can enable me to grow in relationship with Him. And Jesus alone knows how to best accomplish this.

Therefore, it is good for us to look to Jesus and ask Him to grow a close friendship between us and Himself, and then for us to seek Him for this treasure.

Jesus said, "Keep on asking, and you will be given what you

ask for. Keep on looking, and you will find. Keep on knocking, and the door will be opened. For everyone who asks, receives. Everyone who seeks, finds. And the door is opened to everyone who knocks. You parents—if your children ask for a loaf of bread, do you give them a stone instead? Or if they ask for a fish, do you give them a snake? Of course not! If you sinful people know how to give good gifts to your children, how much more will your heavenly Father give good gifts to those who ask him" (Matthew 7:7-11).

It is so important for us to seek Jesus, to ask Him to build our friendship with Him, and to help us to live life as He knows is best for us to do. Writing this book has reminded me what a tremendous privilege it is to have a close friendship with Jesus, the God of the universe! The years I spent as an atheist, out on my own, not knowing why I existed, and being away from God, is so different from what I experience now. I am so thankful that the Ruler of this universe is Jesus and not a distant or malevolent entity, and that Jesus truly has my very best interests at heart—friendship with Him.

If you don't know how to seek Jesus for this, you could start by praying this prayer:

> Please grow in my life a wonderful friendship with You. Please help me to be a very good friend to You. Please help me to know You in a great way. Thanks.

To know Jesus is with us and to have a close friendship with Him are gifts that each of us may receive in different measures. In other words, friendship with Him might come easier to some of us than others. But regardless of the measure we receive, it is always good to ask for a large measure! Because friendship with Jesus is the greatest gift in life, I have asked Him to give me as much of this gift as He is willing to give me, and to enable me to grow in an excellent friendship with Him. If you haven't done so already, I invite you to ask Jesus to give you these same wonderful things.

SECTION 3 – Practical Things We Can Do

This section summarizes and discusses further the practical aspects of growing in our friendship with God. Although most of these items have already been mentioned in this chapter, this section provides a summarized reference.

These ideas are not intended to be a "law," telling us what we must do to have friendship with Jesus. Instead, I hope that we would greatly value doing these things, and that they would be of great benefit to us. So, if you have not done so already, you may want to join me in asking Jesus to teach us how these can best fit into our lives.

I have found the following things to be very helpful in my growing friendship with Jesus. I welcome you to join me in doing these as well.

> **1.** Ask Jesus for:
>
>> **a.** An open heart that is good heart soil.
>>
>> **b.** An infilling of a tremendous measure of Himself (His Holy Spirit). The more we have of Him inside us, the more we will get to know Him and live lives that are pleasing to Him.
>>
>> **c.** A greater realization of His presence.
>>
>> **d.** A strong friendship with Him.
>
> **2.** When Jesus makes something alive to you, look to Him to keep you from hardening your heart (i.e., becoming stiff-necked), so that your heart soil stays fertile for growing in friendship with Him.
>
> **3.** When you wake up in the morning, invite Jesus to join you in your day, and ask Him to help you stay with Him in your

heart throughout the day. Also, periodically give Jesus an extra invitation whenever you go to different places, such as to work or to eat dinner.

4. If possible, spend daily quality alone time with Jesus. Take time to read the Bible, paying close attention to those things that stand out to you, and share your heart with Him.

5. Occasionally take time to silently enjoy Jesus' presence. Take time to pour out your heart to Jesus by sharing with Him your deepest heart's desires and concerns.

6. Take time to have the pond of your heart be cleansed. As I said earlier, I like to do this daily.

7. Whenever you seem to lack the desire to have Jesus first in your life, ask Him to give you the following:

>   **a.** The ability to draw near to Him in your heart.

>   **b.** A greater measure of love in your heart for Him.

>   **c.** The ability to wholeheartedly follow Him.

>   **d.** A heart that places Him first before anything else.

Summary

There is a song, sung by Jonathan Butler (on Kirk Whalum's "The Gospel According to Jazz" Chapter II CD), that has a wonderful line in it, which talks about when someone falls in love with Jesus, it's the best thing they ever did. In this chapter, we have explored some of the keys needed to grow in a deep love-friendship with Jesus, just as Mary did. If Jesus enables us to grow in these things, then it will bring only good effects to our lives.

ENDNOTES

[1]Silverwind, "By His Spirit" (The Sparrow Corporation, 1985), SPC 1096. Used by permission.

Chapter 5 – A Priority of Time

When I graduated from college and entered the job market, I moved to a new town and found that my evenings were filled with lots of free time. For the next few years, I spent a great deal of time reading the Bible (paying special attention to those things that seemed to stand out to me), sharing my heart with God, and journaling my thoughts. When I look back at this time, I realize that this was when my friendship with Jesus really began to blossom.

Later on I married, bought a house, and had children, and I found that my free time shrank considerably. I didn't want to be a negligent parent, so not only did I spend a lot of time with my kids, but I would share my quality time with Jesus with my children. The "quality" aspect of this time considerably decreased and became much more sporadic. So, instead of spending one-and-a-half to two hours a day with Jesus as I had done when I was first out of college, I was only able to spend a little bit of time here and there, and rarely every day.

At first I didn't realize how having less quality time with Jesus was affecting me. But soon I began to notice that my thoughts drifted more quickly toward vacation times and retirement than they ever had before. I began to wonder, *What am I looking for in the extra time that vacation or retirement would provide? Am I missing something in my life?*

As I asked Jesus for wisdom about these questions, I eventually realized that I was missing the fullness of life that I used to have. The real problem was that my spiritual gas tank was low because I rarely "tanked up" in quality alone time with Jesus. It dawned on me that this problem would not be solved through vacation time or retirement, which was still many years away. Instead, I needed to find a way to have more quality alone time with Jesus in my daily life. It occurred to me that if I started taking thirty to forty minutes each night alone with Jesus as soon as the kids went to bed, that would be a good start. As I began to do this almost every night, I found myself starting to "tank up" again. Consistent personal time with God began to saturate my soul, and ironically I found myself improving as a parent as the level of love, patience, and care I had for my children increased. I also found that my desire for vacation times and retirement began to diminish. So, quality, personal time with Jesus began to positively affect my marriage, my parenting, and the rest of my life, as well. It was a striking contrast to what had been occurring, and it showed me what a great need we all have for quality alone time with Jesus.

Through this experience, I learned that it is good to occasionally evaluate how I am using my time. If I am not practical in the use of my time, I can have the deep longing to grow in all the good things I have written about in this book, but yet find that they always tend to get squeezed out of my life by other things.

So if the concepts in this book, such as having good heart soil, learning from God, and growing in friendship with Jesus, have all made sense to you, and you desire to grow in these things because they are pleasing to God, are God's best for you, and are of great benefit to you, then please join me in exploring how we use our time.

In looking at this topic, my desire is not to insult your intelligence. I realize that many of the points in this chapter are straightforward common sense. At the same time, I think it is beneficial for all of us to occasionally evaluate the use of our time so that we can spend it doing those things that are God's best for us.

I realize that you may have a more difficult schedule than I have. You may have an extremely demanding job that requires many hours. You may be a single parent trying to raise kids and make ends meet, and you find yourself constantly run ragged. Whatever your situation, if you haven't done so already, you may want to ask Jesus to give you wisdom on how to have enough quality personal time with Him so that you can be "tanked up" in a way that will positively affect the entirety of your life. Please ask Jesus to cause things to stand out to you as you read this chapter, so that He can show you what would especially be of practical value to you.

Making Time

One thing I've observed about people is that they will make time for whatever they really want to do. If they love to play golf, they'll find time to get out on the greens. If they love to listen to a certain group perform, they'll find the time, energy, and finances to somehow make it to the concerts. In the same way, if someone really wants to grow in their friendship with Jesus, they'll make time to invite Him into their life and spend quality time with Him. Fortunately, if we find this desire to be lacking in us, then we can ask Jesus for a large amount of this good desire and to also open our eyes and see the true value of a quality friendship with Him.

Whose Time Is It?

As I look at how I use my time, the following question has been very helpful: "Does my time belong to me or to Jesus?"

PAUSE POINT

> How do you view your time? Do you view it as belonging to you or to Jesus?

The Bible teaches that our lives are not our own—they belong to Him. This is actually a statement of freedom, guarding us against the temptation to compartmentalize our lives into those areas that we think belong to Jesus, and the rest that we think belong to us to do with as we please. In the long run, it is much more beneficial for us to perceive our lives (including our time) as fully belonging to Jesus and to ask Him for guidance and direction in how best to use them. If we fail to do this, we may be tempted to think that we are getting away with something, but in reality, we are only negatively affecting ourselves and others.

The following verses reinforce that it is best for our time to fully belong to Jesus. When I first read these verses years ago, I struggled with them. I knew that Jesus is completely good and that if He challenges someone, it would only be because He wants what is best for them. Yet I had a hard time understanding His love in these verses that are taken from both Matthew and Luke, which are two parallel passages with slightly different emphasis.

> When Jesus noticed how large the crowd was growing, he instructed his disciples to cross to the other side of the lake.
>
> Then one of the teachers of religious law said to him, "Teacher, I will follow you no matter where you go!"
>
> But Jesus said, "Foxes have dens to live in, and birds have nests, but I, the Son of Man, have no home of my own, not even a place to lay my head."
>
> **Another of his disciples said, "Lord, first let me return home and bury my father."**
>
> **But Jesus told him, "Follow me now! Let those who are spiritually dead care for their own dead"** (Matthew 8:18-22, emphasis mine).
>
> As they were walking along someone said to Jesus, "I will follow you no matter where you go."
>
> But Jesus replied, "Foxes have dens to live in, and birds have nests, but I, the Son of Man, have no home of my own, not even a place to lay my head."
>
> **He said to another person, "Come, be my disciple."**
>
> **The man agreed, but he said, "Lord, first let me return home and bury my father."**

Jesus replied, "Let those who are spiritually dead care for their own dead. Your duty is to go and preach the coming of the Kingdom of God."

Another said, "Yes, Lord, I will follow you, but first let me say good-bye to my family."

But Jesus told him, "Anyone who puts a hand to the plow and then looks back is not fit for the Kingdom of God" (Luke 9:57-62, emphasis mine).

When I first read these verses, I thought, *The man just wanted to go bury his father! Why would Jesus make such a strong statement to him?* But then I wondered if the man had all his time tied up in family and social obligations and, in turn, wasn't free to do what was God's best for him to do. So, in Jesus' love for the man, He challenged him to fully give his time to God. If the man did so, I wouldn't have been surprised if later on Jesus guided him to return and help bury his relative, not out of social obligation, but with God's love flowing through him to his family.

Commitments

If this man truly had all his time tied up in family and social obligations, what commitments had he made? This is a good question to occasionally ask ourselves: "To what have I committed my time?" Many people have a tendency to commit themselves to so many things that their lives are totally consumed with busy schedules. These people might conclude that they are doing what God wants them to do since they are keeping their time commitments, but I've seen people so busy in their schedules that they have no time at all to spend alone with Jesus.

At the beginning of a college semester, there are many things for which a student can sign up—clubs, social events, or intramural sports. But if a student signs up for too many activities, they may find little time left to study. In a similar way, if we are not over committed and we stay less busy, we will be able to spend quality alone time with Jesus, as well as do a quality job in those things to which we are committed.

It is good for us to pray for wisdom in deciding the things to which we should commit ourselves. I try to never make a commitment until I first ask Jesus for wisdom and determine that it seems like the right thing for me to do.

Leisure Time

PAUSE POINT

Please contemplate the following questions about your leisure time.

~ What do you tend to do with your leisure time?

~ Do you consider your leisure time to belong to you or to Jesus?

~ If you do consider your leisure time to belong to Jesus, how can you best use it for His pleasure?

Because leisure time is so important to many of us, we can be easily tempted to compartmentalize it and classify it as **our time** instead of **Jesus' time**. We may not want to give our leisure time to Jesus or ask Him how best to use it. We can easily buy into the idea that we've worked hard at our jobs, our lessons, or our chores, and now we deserve to spend our time in relaxing ways.

It is easy to become "religious" about the things we do in our leisure time. We may feel that it is our right or duty to read the entire newspaper every day, play certain sports, watch certain TV shows, or do the daily crossword puzzle. We can conclude that these activities are our right and we need them to be refreshed, and we may feel bad if we cannot complete one of these activities.

It is very easy to fill up all of our leisure time with such activities and never get around to spending quality time with Jesus. A friend of mine would watch three hours of TV every night, yet found it difficult finding time to spend with Jesus.

However, if we push Jesus out of our leisure time, we will miss out on having our deepened friendship with Him positively affect the rest of our lives. If you have done this but yet have a deep desire to grow in those things that are Jesus' best for you, then you may want to try the following: Share your heart with Jesus and commit all of your leisure time to Him, asking Him for wisdom on how best to use it. Consider spending the first part of your leisure time in quality personal time with Him. This is what my friend eventually decided to do. Rather than watching TV for three hours each night, he took the first hour and spent it with the Lord. That was all that was needed for him to finally have daily time with Jesus. He still watched some TV afterwards, but television no longer came before God.

PAUSE POINT

> How do you think you can be best refreshed as a human being?

Because God knows best how we can be refreshed, it would be good for us to consider what He points us to in the Bible. My spiritual gas tank was on empty until I was finally able to establish some personal time with Jesus almost every day.

> Let the words of Christ [Jesus], in all their richness, live in your hearts and make you wise. Use his words to teach and counsel each other. Sing psalms and hymns and spiritual songs to God with thankful hearts (Colossians 3:16).

The first place for us to be refreshed is in our relationship with Jesus, because this is where our souls will truly be watered. Watching TV and other relaxing activities may provide us with a break from our schedules, and they may even be enjoyable, but they still do not meet the deepest needs of our souls. It is like eating junk food instead of a solid meal. Junk food is fun to eat, but it does not have the same nutritional value as a solid meal. I may not always find my time with Jesus to be refreshing as I immediately begin to read the Bible and share my heart with Him. Sometimes it is like starting a car on a cold day—it takes time for the car to warm up and run smoothly. But the more I am able to consistently take this time with Him, the more I find my heart filling up with His riches. Like money in the bank, it begins to accumulate interest.

Years ago, when I first tried to spend quiet time with Jesus, I found it difficult to keep at it. I often found myself tempted to do other things, such as fall asleep, get something to eat, watch TV, or even vacuum! But by sticking to it, I now find it to be the time in my day to which I look forward the most. What greater privilege could there be than to personally spend time with the magnificent Creator of the universe? How great it is to be with the One who loves me completely! So, if you are finding it difficult to get your spiritual "engine" started, I'd suggest you ask Jesus to help you to have rich times of fellowship with Him.

Quality Personal Time

Throughout this chapter, I have mentioned quality alone time with Jesus, but I realize that this may not always be feasible. When I have gone on some vacations with my family, we have stayed at hotels where there was only one room. At those times, my family has been with me when I take my quality time with Jesus. You may live with your family in a small house or apartment that doesn't allow you to easily find time alone with Jesus. If this is the case, perhaps you can find personal time during your lunch break at work. Whatever your situation, please do not feel that I am laying down a "law" by saying that you must have quality personal time with Jesus without others around. If you ask Him for wisdom, He will guide you into what is best for you to do. My desire is that Jesus would show each of us how best to have quality time with Him.

Practical Things We Can Do

The following is a list of practical things we can do to use our time wisely.

>**1.** Commit all of our time to Jesus.

>**2.** Ask Jesus for the following:

>>**a.** Help to see our schedules as not our own, but belonging to Him, and to see how this can bring real freedom to our lives.

>>**b.** Wisdom and guidance to use our time in a way that is pleasing to Him.

>>**c.** Help to see where we may be unhealthily compartmentalizing our lives, or attempting to lock Him out of those compartments.

>>**d.** Wisdom to commit to the right things.

>>**e.** Help to consistently take time alone with Him and for that time to be truly rich and nurturing to our friendship with Him.

>**3.** Commit all of our leisure time to Jesus, spending the first of that time in quality personal time with Him. During this time, it is good for us to read the Bible, pay special attention to those things that seem to stand out, and share our hearts with Jesus. May this, in turn, positively affect our friendship with Him, as well as the rest of our lives.

Summary

The purpose of this chapter has been to come before God and evaluate our use of time. Mary made it a priority to sit at Jesus' feet, learn from Him, and grow in her friendship with Him, despite her sister's demands to help with the meal preparations. Mary stuck by her priorities, and Jesus commended her for it. My desire is that Jesus would make us wise in the use of our time and in our priorities, and enable us to live lives that are pleasing to Him.

Chapter 6 – Summary

The focus of this book has been to help us live life well at the feet of Jesus, the One who is the center of the universe, the most wonderful, excellent Being we could ever come to know. I'm thankful for the opportunity to share many key concepts to living our lives well at Jesus' feet. Hopefully you have heard what Jesus has wanted to say to you through this book, and He has given you wisdom on how best to apply these things in your life.

There is value and freedom in these key concepts:

~ Daily picking up our crosses and following Jesus.

~ Putting the entirety of our lives on God's altar.

~ Keeping our minds and hearts cleansed, and maintaining soft and open hearts before Jesus.

~ Learning from Jesus in all of life.

~ Growing in close friendship with Jesus, daily inviting Him to be with us, and asking Him to help us to be with Him through the day.

~ Being wise in our use of time.

If you are learning from Jesus and growing in your friendship with Him, then He will continue to bring you into His very best for your life.

Practical Things We Can Do

Before closing, I'd like to list two final practical suggestions.

1. On your own, you may want to take a final review of the sections titled "Practical Things We Can Do," found near the end of Chapters 3 through 5. Before reading these sections, please ask Jesus to give you a sense of how He thinks these things are working in your life. May He then cause things to stand out to you and give you a sense of any changes that would be good for you to make.

2. Please join me in re-reading this book every year or two, in order to keep focused on the things that will help us continue to live our lives well at Jesus' feet.

Thank you for allowing me to share my heart with you through this book. My desire for you is the same desire I have for myself—that Jesus' very best would come forth beautifully in our lives.

Appendix – Further Ideas on How to Read and Study the Bible

Earlier in this book, I suggested that we ask God to teach us in all of life and take time to read the Bible daily. As we ask God to teach us in all of life, when we read the Bible, God will most likely make certain things stand out to us. If we pause and contemplate those things, it can be amazing how God will help us to see how those things pertain to what we are currently going through in our daily lives.

If you have never read the Bible before, you may find the following reading path to be helpful. This is the path I took when I first read the Bible. If you already read the Bible, but would like a new reading path, then I welcome you to try it as well.

1. Read the book of John, and then the entire New Testament (Matthew through Revelation).

2. Read the New Testament two more times.

3. Put three bookmarks in the Bible: one in the Old Testament (Genesis through Malachi), one in the Gospels (Matthew through John), and one in the rest of the New Testament (Acts through Revelation). Each time you sit down to read, read one chapter from the section behind each bookmark. When your bookmark hits the end of a section, just move it back to the beginning. For example, when you reach the end of the book of John, put the bookmark back at the beginning of the book of Matthew.

4. When your first bookmark reaches the end of the Old Testament book of Malachi, then either repeat step 3 or go on to step 5.

5. Put five bookmarks in the Bible: two that divide the Old Testament, one in the Gospels, and two that divide the rest of the New Testament:

> Bookmark 1 – Genesis through Job
>
> Bookmark 2 – Psalms through Malachi
>
> Bookmark 3 – Matthew through John
>
> Bookmark 4 – Acts through Ephesians
>
> Bookmark 5 – Philippians through Revelation

Each time you sit down to read, read one chapter from the sections behind bookmarks 1, 3, and 4. The next time you read, read from the sections behind bookmarks 2, 3, and 5. When bookmark 1 gets to the end of Job, wait until bookmark 2 gets to the end of Malachi. Then move both bookmarks 1 and 2 to their beginning points of Genesis and Psalms (since you have just completed reading the Old Testament). When bookmark 3 gets to the end of John, move it to the beginning of Matthew (since you have just completed reading the Gospels). When bookmark 4 gets to the end of Ephesians, wait until bookmark 5 gets to the end of Revelation. Then move both bookmarks 4 and 5 to their beginning points of Acts and Philippians (since you have just completed reading the New Testament).

6. Try other things, such as reading different Bible translations or moving your bookmarks in different ways. For example, you could read an entire book of the Bible at one bookmark before moving to read an entire book at your next bookmark, and so forth.

I have found this reading path to be of real value to me, and I truly believe that God directed me to read His Word in this way. After reading through the Bible many times, I realize some of the reasons why.

If I simply open the Bible and read on whatever page it opens to, I have occasionally found a verse or passage that has been just what I needed at that point in time. But if this is my only way of reading the Bible, it would be difficult for me to gain a fuller understanding of the entire Bible. It is like reading any book: I may want to skim the book or read the summary before reading it from cover to cover. But if all I do is skim the book or read the summary, I will never gain a full understanding of the book. It would also make it more difficult to consistently read the book, because I will never know when I have completed it. Having a reading path that takes me through the whole Bible has helped me to stay consistent in reading it almost every day.

The Gospels (Matthew, Mark, Luke, and John) focus especially on Jesus. And because Jesus is God, watching Him interact with others will give us insight into how God interacts with people, including showing us what He likes and dislikes. The reading path I have provided begins with the Gospels and places the heaviest concentration of reading on them.

Many things in the Old Testament (Genesis through Malachi) make sense in light of the New Testament (Matthew through Revelation), so I'm glad I read the New Testament a few times before I started to read the Old Testament. Also, when using the three or five bookmark system, I wind up with a greater concentration of reading in the New Testament than in the Old Testament.

Lastly, one reason I suggest to eventually place bookmarks at different places in the Bible is that different parts of the Bible have different focuses. It's like a meal that consists of different foods, such as meat, potatoes, salad, vegetables, bread, and dessert. I like to "eat" from different areas of the Bible for a varied and well-balanced spiritual diet. If a chapter at one bookmark seems a little dry, often sections at the other bookmarks wind up being quite tasty.

Summary for *Four in One*

Now that you have read all four books contained in **Four in One**, we hope it is easy for you to see how they all tie together and work together to make this single book.

We also hope you enjoyed **Four in One** and that the book material came alive to you through the invisible working of the Holy Spirit in your life!

Lastly, we hope that each time you read **Four in One**, that Jesus touches your life every single time and that it all the more helps you to have a wonderful friendship with Him and with others too – that continue on for eternity in Heaven some day!

With Jesus' love,

Scott and Bonna Brooks

CPSIA information can be obtained
at www.ICGtesting.com
Printed in the USA
BVOW11s1412210517
484714BV00002B/4/P